FORTY-NINE STEPS
TO GREATNESS

FORTY-NINE STEPS TO GREATNESS

*A day-to-day plan for
success through
Torah learning*

Ephraim Nisenbaum

A TARGUM PRESS Book

First published 2007
Copyright © 2007 by Ephraim Nisenbaum
ISBN 978-1-56871-429-5

Published by:
TARGUM PRESS, INC.
22700 W. Eleven Mile Rd.
Southfield, MI 48034
E-mail: targum@targum.com
Fax: 888-298-9992
www.targum.com

Distributed by:
FELDHEIM PUBLISHERS
208 Airport Executive Park
Nanuet, NY 10954

Printing plates by Frank, Jerusalem
Printed in Israel by Chish

Comments may be directed to the author at enisenbaum@aol.com.

אברהם חיים לוין
RABBI AVROHOM CHAIM LEVIN
5104 N. Drake Avenue • Chicago, IL 60625
ROSH HAYESHIVA/TELSHE-CHICAGO • ראש הישיבה\טלז-שיקגו

ב"ה

הרם בא'ו"ר ל' ל' היה הכ"ה

ב'ד"י הרב הגא"ן ר' אברהם וי'ס)קדוש שי'(ו
הלו' מתאבלו'נ'ש לאש'(ו הי'מגו', וכדר
כאה גו'ע אחו/ רב שמרו(ש ושרג ואפ'ע
גדו/ל כ'יר ק'יון ל'ו'ג וי' א' כ'רין דן
לאסו' שפרי' ה)מ"עו לארחת" האפ
וכ'א דרגת ל'הרה ס' ספר ל'ארחת הא
וי)א'ע' הקל)סרסע זהב אל ה'וא'ש
תרוה ותרא'ה יהל'א אש'ם אל"יא זכ'
והו' גכ ש'תקות ו'ורות ולהרבת הש
כחו' תאג'ן דהכ)ות ד'רי ה)ל) ואאמא
ורה'ם יקהל" ת'רה ואו'א אפסרי.
וא'תדרך ש'ן הא'ות ל'אש'י ש'
ל'או' ג' ו'ו' וא'גן ו'אור ו'ורא
ל'הו' פ'ע' א' הרדע . וי'ג' ה)אחבו דכ'
אודרהא תש' ה)ו' ק'ו' ו"ן

RABBI SHMUEL DISHON
1682 48th Street
Brooklyn, NY

יום ב לפי ויחי התשס״ז

לכבוד הר״ר אפרים ניסנבוים שיחי לאי״ט,

I was very happy to see your book on the 48 *kinyanim*. The 48 *kinyanim* are an important step needed for a person to be able to *shteig* in *limud haTorah* and we must familiarize ourselves with them. Your book explains each *kinyan* clearly according to the different *mefarshim*, while showing real-life examples from our *gedolei Torah asher mipihem anu chayim*, both in our generation and from earlier generations. The short and simple style will also make it easier for people to learn one of the *kinyanim* each day and implement them in their lives. This is especially appropriate for the *yemei hasefirah* which are *mesugal* to learn the 48 *kinyanim*. The *Ribbono shel Olam* should grant you *berachah* and *hatzlachah* and you should be *zocheh* that your book be *mashpia* others in their *aliyah baTorah u'veyirah*.

בידידות,
שמואל דישון

In Loving Memory of

מרדכי בן ר׳ אפרים

חנה בת ר׳ יעקב אייזיק

אברהם בן צבי אלימלך הלוי

חשא בת יצחק איסר

By their children
and grandchildren

IN LOVING MEMORY OF

ISRAEL AND NAOMI COMET

ר ישראל בן ר׳ יעקב אייזיק ז״ל

נחמה בת הרב משה ליב ע״ה

Champions of Torah in Cleveland and Israel

FAYE COMET

פיגא בת שמואל ע״ה

A woman of dedication and dignity

CONTENTS

THE FORTY-NINE ESSENTIAL QUALITIES FOR ACQUIRING TORAH

FOREWORD

Letter from HaRav Mattisyahu Salomon, shlita
Mashgiach of Beth Medrash Govoha, Lakewood, NJ

לכבוד ידידי הרה"ג כמוה"ר אפרים ניסנבוים שליט"א
נהניתי מאד מהכתבים על מ"ח קניני התורה ובמקום הסכמה הנני
שולח הערה כוללת על קנין אחרונה מעלת האומר דבר בשם אומרו.

בכבוד ובהערכה,
מתתי' חיים סלומון

In place of a *haskamah*, I am sending you an insight into the forty-eighth quality needed in order to acquire Torah, *ha'omer davar b'shem omro*, citing one's sources.

How strange, that after all the forty-seven special attributes we have to work so hard to make part of our character in order to become a "possessor" of the Torah, we still need to acquire what seems to be just a minor detail, and, at that, quite an easy one. To be particular to say over Torah insights in the name of the one from whom we heard it does not seem so difficult, or even so important. Why was just this quality chosen to round off all the *kinyanei Torah*?

The truth is that this is not such a small detail, nor is it so easy. One has to be very humble, very honest, and very aware how much of our knowledge and information is not the product of our own mind or our own observation, but has been transmitted to us by our parents, teachers, and friends.

There is a terrific *yetzer hara* to want to make out as if we are the clever ones, and it is very difficult for us to admit that, really, all we are doing is repeating something that we have heard from someone else. It takes all the pleasure out of our discussion or conversation!

For this reason we are given here a special incentive — no less than to "bring the redemption to the whole world!" Isn't it worth it! To forego that passing pleasure of feeling good, to relinquish a moment of masquerading as an inventor of ideas, and rather to be honest to admit that no one owes us any *kavod* for these ideas which are not our own, and then enjoy the permanent pleasure of bringing the *geulah*. Can we imagine the satisfying feeling of people who know that, by the way they conducted their discussions, redemption came to the world? Is this not a fair compensation?

But how does it work? Merely to say over in another person's name can actually bring the *geulah*? Have not people done this before and the redemption has not yet arrived? The Maharal in his explanation makes two very important remarks. Firstly he says, we are not only speaking of the *ge'ulah sheleimah*, the complete redemption of *yemos HaMashiach*. Even if the time of the complete redemption has not yet been reached, nevertheless an easing of our situation will take place, and every bit easier things become for us in *galus* is considered a redemption of sorts.

Secondly, the connection between *geulah* and *omer davar*

b'shem omro is explained by the Maharal in this way. Hashem Yisbarach is always prepared to ease our situation in *galus*, but only if we are prepared to recognize how helpless and useless we are without His Divine assistance. Only if we are prepared to declare that He does everything, and we will never take the credit for any improvement in our situation, nor attribute it to our own might and strength, will we merit the *geulah*. Each time we cite the source of an insight or idea, we are training ourselves in this trait; we are habituating ourselves to recognizing the True Source of all goodness, the Source of our Redemption.

ACKNOWLEDGMENTS

"Katonti mikol hachasadim asher asisa es avdecha"
(Bereishis 32:11).

To paraphrase the words of our forefather Yaakov, I am humbled by all the great kindness Hashem has showered upon me, and especially in allowing me to publish this book, my third *sefer, b'ezras Hashem.* I am most grateful for the opportunity to do my little part in spreading Torah amongst our people.

I hope that my efforts will find favor in Hashem's eyes, and He will allow me to continue learning and teaching Torah for many years to come.

Most of the material presented in this *sefer* has been gleaned from the classic commentaries on *Avos,* such as *Midrash Shmuel,* the Maharal's *Derech Chaim,* Rav Yaakov Emden's *Lechem Shamayim,* and *Tiferes Yisrael. Cheshev HaEfod,* a contemporary, thorough work on the forty-eight *kinyanim* by Rabbi Eliezer Poll, was also very helpful. The stories and anecdotes were taken from various sources. I am especially indebted to Rav Moshe Levi for kindly permitting me to reprint many, perhaps even most, of the stories and vignettes from his *Mishel HaAvos,* a beautiful, three-volume anthology on the

15

forty-eight *kinyanim*. Rabbi Dr. Abraham Twerski's *Visions of the Fathers* and *Kuntres Alei Be'er* by Rav Yosef Ben-Amram were also helpful. My appreciation is also due to HaRav Mattisyahu Salomon, *shlita*, for his kind words and for his contribution of a piece on the the forty-eighth *kinyan*.

The world recently lost one of the foremost *ba'alei mussar*, thinkers, and educators of our time, with the passing of the Mashgiach, HaRav Shlomo Wolbe, *z"l*. Although I was privileged to learn directly under Rav Wolbe for only a short period of time, his wise and quiet encouragement has affected my entire life. I am extremely grateful for the time I was fortunate to spend with him in Yeshivas Be'er Yaakov and in Yerushalayim, and his influence continues to guide me. The Mashgiach once wrote to a young *bachur* that although they could not converse regularly, whenever the *bachur* would learn Rav Wolbe's *sefer*, *Alei Shur*, it would be as if the Mashgiach was speaking to him directly (*Igros U'Kesavim*, p. 2). I, too, still feel his presence in my life, and I hope that in some small way, this *sefer*, inspired in part by a personal discussion with the Mashgiach, will be a source of *nachas ruach* for his *neshamah*.

I am also most fortunate to have enjoyed, and continue to enjoy, a wonderful relationship with my Roshei Yeshivah at Telshe Yeshivah, Chicago. HaRav Avraham Chaim Levin, *shlita*, HaRav Chaim Dov Keller, *shlita*, and *lihibadel bein chaim l'chaim*, HaRav Chaim Schmelczer, *z"l*, have been much more than *rebbeim*. I owe them a tremendous debt of gratitude for everything I have been able to accomplish.

A person gains immeasurably from his friends. Be they words of encouragement or of criticism, our personalities and achievements benefit from both. I feel fortunate to have benefited so much from my friends and students. I appreciate the insightful comments on this book from Rabbi Yitzchak Miller, Sam Harris, my dear son-in-law Rabbi Laibel Yellin, and from Rabbi Dovid Goldwasser. This work gained tremendously from the expertise of Ms. Jill Brotman, who critically edited the manuscript, providing much needed style and clarity. May she enjoy good health and *nachas*. Mr. David Kahn's insights were also very helpful. My sincere thanks, too, to my daughter Malkie, for her editing and proofreading.

Targum Press has gained a well-deserved reputation for excellence in the Jewish publishing world. Their professionalism and sensitivity in all areas is truly a *kiddush Hashem*. I am especially grateful to Mrs. Avigail Sharer and to D.Liff for helping create a beautiful work. Many thanks are also due Rabbi Moshe Dombey, *z"l*, founder of Targum Press, for his confidence in this book. His passing is a loss for *klal Yisrael*.

I would like to express my appreciation to my parents, Reb Yaakov and Karen Nisenbaum, *sheyichiyu*, for all their wisdom, love, and support. They have always been role models for me to emulate. Their love of Torah and *chesed*, their complete submission before *da'as Torah*, and their sincere love and devotion to their family, are truly impressive. May they enjoy the fruits of all their labors for many years together, in good health and *simchah*.

My parents-in-law, Rav Chaim Zvi and Gittel Goldzweig, *sheyichiyu*, are also mentors, not only to their family, but to people around the world. Their selfless *chesed, ahavas haTorah*, and feelings of responsibility to *klal Yisrael* are legendary. It is an honor to be part of their family. May HaKadosh Baruch Hu grant them both many years of good health and *nachas* from the entire family.

I am eternally indebted to the Almighty for all the blessings He has bestowed upon me, and especially the blessing of my dear wife Chanie *shetichiyeh* and our children *sheyichiyu*. I am inspired and humbled by my wife's selfless devotion to our children and to me, and she truly deserves much of the credit for anything I have been fortunate enough to accomplish. May the Almighty grant us the good health and strength to serve Him well, and to merit seeing our children do the same.

INTRODUCTION

Authors will often relate what inspired them to put their thoughts to paper. I am almost embarrassed to admit how this book came to be written. I run an educational program for adults, many of whom have not had much previous exposure to Torah. When teaching about Torah and mitzvos, I always try to focus on the practical understanding of the mitzvos, and how the observance of mitzvos can foster spiritual growth.

During the *yom tov* seasons we always try to examine the theme of the *yom tov*, and we discuss how we can each personally experience the theme and meaning of the day. Many of my students at the Jewish Learning Connection are eager to hear practical suggestions how they may harness the energy of a *yom tov*, and they never fail to interrogate me about my own success in implementing these suggestions.

During the period of *sefiras ha'omer*, the seven weeks between Pesach and Shavuos, I always explain the connection between the forty-nine days and the forty-eight ways of preparing oneself to receive the Torah on Shavuos. Inevitably I am asked,

Introduction

"Rabbi, do *you* work on a specific character trait each day during the *omer?*" Unfortunately, I cannot say that I am either sufficiently disciplined or inspired to always do so.

This admission has pushed me into some serious introspection and to ponder several questions. Is it fair for me to talk about a link that may be fostered between the *omer* and self-improvement, if I myself have no practical program for doing so? Is it hypocritical for me to expect others to practice what I may not do myself? Could a practical program inspire and encourage me (as well as my students) to take advantage of the opportunities afforded during these seven weeks? And, if it could work during the period of the *omer*, could it also be implemented at other times throughout the year?

These questions have led me to formulate a program that offers practical guidance. The format is short and simple, yet it is comprehensive. It is designed to be studied and applied on each day of the *omer*, or during any seven-week period throughout the year. *Forty-nine Steps to Greatness* is based on the writings of the *ba'alei mussar*, students of Rav Yisrael Salanter's program for ethical development, and other great teachers of the past several centuries. Although the book was written primarily to inspire and encourage me to take advantage of the great opportunities afforded during the weeks of the *omer*, if it will inspire anybody else to do the same anytime during the year, it will more than have accomplished its purpose.

Regarding the mitzvah of *sefiras ha'omer*, the Torah instructs us: "You shall count for yourselves from the morrow of the Shabbos [Pesach], from the day you bring the *omer* offering, seven complete weeks; until the morrow of the seventh week, you shall count fifty days"[1] (*Vayikra* 23:15–16). The Torah does

1 The Torah instructs us to count fifty days, but the fiftieth day is Shavuos itself. Therefore, only forty-nine days, or seven weeks, are counted between Pesach and Shavuos.

not give any reason for counting these days, nor does it explain the significance of doing so. The *ba'alei mussar* say that these days are meant for preparing ourselves to receive the Torah on Shavuos. But how are we supposed to prepare for receiving the Torah? And why do we need forty-nine days to do so?

The Alter of Kelm, Rav Simcha Zissel Ziv (*Chochmah U'Mussar*, vol.1, ch. 236), suggests a connection between the forty-nine days and the forty-eight ways through which the Torah is acquired, as listed in *Avos* 6:6.[1] In order for us to be able to acquire the Torah on Shavuos, we must first master forty-eight character traits. Each day of the *omer* corresponds to one of the forty-eight characteristics that serves as the guide for that day's preparations. On the forty-ninth day, we strive to link all the achievements, or characteristics, together. Only then are we ready to receive the Torah.

One more thing must first be understood: How are we able to do this in only seven weeks? As Rav Yisrael Salanter explains, successful self-improvement through learning *mussar* can only be realized after constant repetition and over a long period of time (*Ohr Yisrael*, ch. 20). Generally speaking, we must work a long time to develop a desirable character trait,[2] particularly to make it part of our nature. How can we possibly refine our character in such a short period of time?

Several explanations have been suggested. First, Rav Shlomo Wolbe[3] draws a distinction between the *avodah* of pre-

---

1   Although the sixth chapter of *Avos* is usually printed as part of the *maseches*, it is actually an independent *beraisa*, often referred to as *Perek Kinyan Torah*.

2   Rav Yisrael Salanter once said that it is easier to master the entire Talmud than it is to master one character trait. Rav Mordechai Gifter, the Telzer Rosh Yeshivah, added that it is noteworthy this adage was made by someone who had personally mastered both! (I heard this from Rav Gifter)

3   Rav Wolbe's comments were made during a personal discussion.

paring to receive the Torah and that of rectifying bad character traits. Ordinarily, it takes a great investment of effort and time to develop good character. However, to acquire the character sufficient for receiving the Torah, a less rigorous exercise is required. As long as we identify our goals and what is needed to accomplish them — and then make a concerted effort towards that end — Hashem agrees to entrust us with His Torah.

Rav Elya Lopian compares the acquisition of Torah to a material acquisition. As long as a partial payment is made, proving his good intentions and sincerity, one can acquire a material object before paying the total purchase price. Similarly, one may also merit to receive the Torah with a "partial acquisition," or partial attainment, of the forty-eight qualities worked on during the corresponding days.

In the pages that follow, a short description of each of the forty-eight attributes is presented and illustrated with anecdotal material culled from the rich legacy of our great leaders through the generations, who have mastered these attributes. Practical points for their application are also given. It is recommended that each day, one read only the section for the corresponding day during the *omer*, and then spend a little time reflecting how the trait could be implemented. Reading more than one section at a time could distract from one's focus and resolve to improve in that day's quality. On the last day of the *omer, erev Shavuos*, one should review all forty-eight qualities. Of course, as mentioned, the program may be implemented at any other time of the year, too.

May we merit the capability of implementing these suggestions, and thereby be deserving of Hashem's holy Torah.

The Forty-Nine Essential Qualities for Acquiring Torah

1 STUDY

תלמוד

To acquire Torah, it is obviously necessary to first study it. We can hardly gain skills or knowledge for life if we know little about what we wish to acquire. Moreover, Torah study is considered such a great mitzvah that the Mishnah states, "The study of Torah is the equivalent of all the other mitzvos" (*Pe'ah* 1:1). Only through knowledge of Torah can we observe it properly.

The Rambam rules that a person must study Torah regularly until the day he dies (*Hilchos Talmud Torah* 1:5). It makes no difference whether one is healthy or ill, young or old, wealthy or poor; there is never an exemption from studying, for Torah study is the source of life. The Talmud compares the Jewish people's dependence on Torah study to the fish's need for water. Just as a fish cannot survive out of the water, a Jew cannot survive in the absence of Torah study (*Avodah Zarah* 3b).

In order to utilize every available minute for Torah study, it is important to value and organize one's time appropriately. In fact, the Alter of Kelm, Rav Simchah Zissel Ziv, instituted a five-minute study session for his students specifically so that they would learn to value every moment properly and use it for Torah study.

✦ The *daf yomi* program, in which each participant studies a *daf* (folio) of Talmud each day, has encouraged regular Talmud study throughout the world. Sometimes, a little ingenuity is called for, such as when a group of commuters from Long Island to Manhattan encountered difficulty finding the time to cover the daily material. Then they realized how much valuable time was being wasted in their daily commute to and from work. Thus was born the Long Island railroad train *daf yomi shiur*, for which a sizeable group of men meets each day in the same train car.

✦ ✦ ✦

✦ The Chasam Sofer, one of the leading Torah luminaries of his generation, was once asked by a childhood friend, "What does it take to become a truly great scholar? What was the difference between you and the other students in our class, that you achieved such greatness?"

"It takes only five minutes to become great!" the Chasam Sofer replied. "A person who makes use of all his spare time to study Torah, five minutes here, and a few extra minutes there, will undoubtedly become a great scholar. I tried to make sure that I used all of my 'five minutes,' and that's how I accomplished what I did."

It is not sufficient to study Torah by oneself. One must study with a *rebbi* or teacher. This is included in the attribute of *talmud*, study (see *Tiferes Yisrael; Derech Chaim;* and *HaChassid Ya'avetz*). The teacher can guide one in his studies, provide clarification, and help one avoid misunderstanding.

The obligation to study Torah every day includes study both in the morning and in the evening, as it says, "You shall delve into it both by day and by night" (*Yehoshua* 1:8; see also *Tanchuma, Beshalach* 20).

Rav Elya Meir Bloch, the Rosh Yeshivah of Telshe-Cleveland, made a commitment to learn at least one hour a day, come what may.[1] Since he was responsible for the yeshivah's financial burden, at times he would return home late at night after a gruelling day of fundraising. Nonetheless, he made sure to get his hour of study before retiring for the night. Even at the end of his life, when he was in too much pain to concentrate, he had a student learn aloud in his hospital room so that he could absorb whatever Torah learning possible. One of the main features of our Torah giants is their commitment to Torah study, come what may.

Plan: ✦ *Make an effort to take Torah study seriously, ensuring a Torah study session every day (the length of this session is obviously dependent on the scope of one's activities and responsibilities), however, it should be a serious session).*

✦ *Establish and maintain a meaningful relationship with a rebbi or teacher, from whom one can learn Torah and accept guidance.*

---

1 When officiating at weddings, HaRav Chaim Stein, *shlita*, the Telzer Rosh Yeshivah, always encourages the *chasan* to accept a similar resolution upon himself.

2 ATTENTIVE LISTENING

שמיעת האוזן

When one learns from a teacher, or even from a friend, it is necessary to pay attention to each word that is being taught (*Midrash Shmuel; Derech Chaim*). This is especially true regarding instruction in Torah, because the wording of the Torah is so concise and precise. Sometimes, missing a single sentence, detail, or just one word, can change the entire context and meaning of what is being taught, leading to a serious misunderstanding. Carried a step further, this can result in improper observance by the student or by anyone who learns from the student. Ultimately, a breakdown of the *mesorah*, the intergenerational transmission of the Torah, can occur.

Being attentive shows that one is making a concerted effort to listen carefully to what is being said, and that he doesn't want to miss any of the details. A devoted baseball fan can rattle off all the "stats" of his favorite team and knows the batting average of each player, the number of runs batted in and homeruns scored. He pays careful attention to these details, because they interest him. A true interest in Torah is also expressed in attention to detail.

Rav Elchanan Wasserman once commented that there is a major distinction between success in Torah learning and success in other areas of knowledge. To achieve greatness in medicine or science, for example, one must be blessed with a sharp mind and considerable talent. To achieve greatness in Torah, however, all that is required is an attentive mind and the desire to excel (*Kovetz Ma'amorim*).

✦ Rav Simcha Zissel Broide, the late Rosh Yeshivah of Yeshivas Chevron, recalled his own experience in the yeshivah, how Rav Nosson Tzvi Finkel, the Alter of Slabodka, would deliver a discourse. The Alter would speak very softly. The students would crowd around, leaning precariously on their *shtenders*, eager to hear every word. The stillness of the room would occasionally be broken by the sound of a *shtender* falling to the floor, its owner obviously having leaned too far over. Yet still the students continued to lean, straining their ears to hear the Alter's words of Torah, hanging on to every word the Alter uttered.

✦ ✦ ✦

✦ Rav Elchanan Wasserman was the Chafetz Chaim's premier student. A Torah giant in his own right, each year he would leave his own yeshivah in Baranovich and travel to spend Rosh HaShanah with his *rebbi*. One year, after the Chafetz Chaim finished delivering words of inspiration to the yeshivah, Rav Shalom Eishishoker leaned over to Reb Elchanan and whispered, "I think he said the exact same thing last year." Reb Elchanan whispered back, "No, this year there were eight words different!"

Rav Tzvi Pesach Frank expands on this quality. He points out that one should not only listen carefully to the words of his teacher, but that he should also listen to what he himself is saying as he studies. This is closely related to the next essential quality for studying Torah: articulate speech, or, studying aloud. Listening to the words one is saying, paying attention to those words, is a great help in understanding the material clearly, because it helps one focus and concentrate (cited in *Mishel HaAvos*).

Plan: ✦ *Pay closer attention to shiurim and chavrusos, listening carefully to each word and every nuance.*

3 ARTICULATE SPEECH
עריכת שפתים

orah should not be studied silently, as is common with other subjects. The Talmud states that only Torah that is studied aloud can be absorbed into one's being (*Eiruvin* 54a). Torah that is studied silently does not make as great an impression on one's mind; thus, it is easily forgotten.

People are accustomed to seeing serious study in the quiet of study halls and libraries. Entering the *beis midrash* of a yeshivah for the first time, they are usually in for a shock, as it sounds nothing like a library. Rather, one is greeted by an explosion of noise. Young men are humming, singing, and reviewing their studies out loud. It's hard to imagine that one could concentrate with so much noise, yet it is in these surroundings, in the midst of the cacophony, that Torah is acquired.[1]

The *Shulchan Aruch HaRav* rules that one does not even

---

1 However, see *Tiferes Yisrael* on *Avos* 1:15, *Boaz* 2, who distinguishes between one's own learning out loud and learning in a noisy room. He suggests learning in a quiet room.

fulfill the mitzvah of Torah study unless he speaks out the words — similar to prayer, which also requires the words to be enunciated (*Talmud Torah* 2:12). (He adds, however, that when one is concentrating deeply, he need not enunciate the words.)

✦ When Rav Elchanan Wasserman would prepare for his *shiurim*, he would say each line of the Gemara aloud and translate it word by word into Yiddish, as if he was explaining it to a young student. If he came across a difficult passage, he would formulate the question, and ponder it for a few minutes. He would then study the section a second time, and again ask the question. He repeated the process a third and fourth time. When the subject became clear, he would ask himself, "So what have we said now?" and summarize what had been covered.

Sefer Alei Be'er expounds on the verse, "then this song shall speak up before it as witness, that it shall not be forgotten from the mouth of its children..."(*Devarim* 31:21). He explains that only when the Torah is like a song — when it is sung aloud and with joy — is it certain that it will not be forgotten. *Tiferes Yisrael* (*Erachin* 4:1, *Boaz*) suggests that the *mishnayos* were originally sung to specific tunes, in order to make them easier to remember by heart.

Midrash Shmuel also explains that the Torah must be fluent on one's lips, and in order to achieve this one must constantly review his studies. In fact, without review it is easy to forget everything one has learned. One who studies Torah but does not review his studies is compared to one who plants but does not reap the fruits of his labor (*Sanhedrin* 99a).

Elsewhere, the Talmud states that a student who only reviews his lesson one hundred times cannot be compared to a student who reviews his lesson one hundred and one times (*Chagigah* 9b). The more one reviews, the easier it is to remember the Torah, and the clearer his knowledge will be.

✦ Rav Chaim Shmulevitz, the Mirrer Rosh Yeshivah, studied with a *chavrusa* late each night. Once, during the course of their learning, Reb Chaim discussed several ways of understanding the *sugya* they were learning. The following night, Reb Chaim off-handedly repeated each approach they had discussed the previous night. His *chavrusa* was amazed. "How did you remember the entire discussion so clearly?" he asked.

"What did you do last night after we had finished?" Reb Chaim asked.

"Why, I went to sleep. It was already late," his *chavrusa* replied.

"When I got home," Reb Chaim said, "I also climbed into bed. But then I buried my head in my pillow and went over our entire discussion, shouting out the different arguments over and over again, for a couple of hours, until each one was etched indelibly in my mind. Is it any wonder that I can remember what we said last night?"

✦ ✦ ✦

✦ A scholar once complained to Rav Refael Shapiro of Volozhin that he had reviewed an entire tractate several times, but still felt he didn't remember it clearly enough.

Rav Shapiro smiled and said, "After several times you expect to remember the tractate well? As far as I'm concerned, until I have studied something fifteen times, it's merely been learned. Only what I study after the fifteenth time do I consider to be review. You must review the tractate many times in order to know it well."

Plan: ✦ *Study Torah out loud and review each lesson several times at least, to ensure good retention.*

4 AN UNDERSTANDING HEART

בינת הלב

Can you imagine an elementary school child using a law school textbook in a sixth grade? Yet, the same *Bava Metzia* can be discussed on an elementary level as well as on a much deeper level. It is fascinating that when young children are first introduced to Torah study, they use the very same text of *Chumash* or Talmud as does the great and established scholar. Torah can be studied and understood on many levels. The magnitude of Torah is referred to as being "like the heights of the heavens...deeper than the greatest depth...longer than the earth, and wider than the sea" (*Iyov* 11:8–9).

The acquisition of Torah requires much more than a cursory understanding of Torah. An understanding heart means that one must make a concerted effort to delve deeply into and analyze the intricacies of every nuance and detail of Torah

(*Derech Chaim*). The Chazon Ish is reported to have said that an accomplished scholar is one who can cover eighty pages of Talmud in one day, as well as one page of Talmud in eighty days.

✦ An established *talmid chacham* in Slabodka studied with a student who was very wordly. The student once challenged his mentor with a question regarding a geographical description in the Talmud that didn't match the map of the world. Later, the mentor remarked to Rav Yaakov Kaminetzky in disgust, "How does someone ask a question on the Torah from a map?"

Reb Yaakov disagreed vehemently. "Of course the map must coincide with Torah! If Torah is true, how could it contradict what we see on the map? The question deserves our attention and must be clarified!" Reb Yaakov worked on the problem until he answered it successfully.

✦ ✦ ✦

✦ A childhood friend of Rav Baruch Ber Leibovitz, Rosh Yeshivah of Kaminetz, recalled their years together under Rav Chaim Brisker. "Reb Baruch Ber would spend endless hours analyzing each of Reb Chaim's insights. We felt Reb Baruch Ber was making a mistake, that he should be spending more time covering ground. In retrospect, however, although many prominent rabbis and scholars emerged from that group, there is only one Reb Baruch Ber. A Torah giant the caliber of a Rav Baruch Ber is only the result of the most intensive learning."

Rabbi Abraham Twerski offers an insight regarding the expression "an understanding heart." What does understanding have to do with the heart? he asks. The heart is thought to be the seat of the emotions, not the seat of the intellect. He suggests that it is from the heart, from the emotions, that bias may emerge to impair our judgment and distort our understanding. Our understanding must be secure, not only in our minds, but in our hearts as well. This requires not only study, but also a thorough and honest examination of our intentions. This may be why the Talmud (*Eiruvin* 13b) relates that when the school of Hillel would disagree with that of Shammai, they would always cite Shammai's opinion before their own. They wanted to ensure that their bias did not cloud their presentation of the two opinions.

✦ Rav Shach was once speaking to a group of yeshivah students. "If you were ninety-nine years old, had just endured a painful circumcision, and now saw three dusty idolators traveling in the wilderness, it's very possible you would run towards them and offer them a place to rest and a meal. After all, that is exactly what we learn about our ancestor Avraham (*Bereishis* 18:11-20). Then how is it, that yeshivah students sit at the table when a new student appears, and they don't run to greet him with offers to sit down and to bring him food? Students understand what a *kal v'chomer* is, yet they don't see that if a ninety-nine year old invalid runs to help three idolators, certainly young and healthy students should help another Jew! That is only because they learn the Torah's account with their mind and not their heart."

Plan: ✦ *Eliminate any subjective bias that might distort proper understanding.*
✦ *Study Torah in greater depth, concentrating on understanding the meaning behind every word and detail.*

5 AN INTELLIGENT HEART[1]

שכלות הלב

Rav Yaakov Emden explains that an "intelligent heart" is a notch above an "understanding heart." One must use intelligence to ascertain that every insight and interpretation is firmly rooted in Torah sources. All the ramifications of an insight must be understood, and the reasoning must be carefully followed to a logical conclusion. The outcome must then be gauged according to Torah law (*Lechem Shamayim*).

◆ Rav Yechezkel Abramsky, author of *Chazon Yechezkel*, once remarked that it is not very difficult to come up with a *chiddush*. The difficult part is to examine one's new insight against any contradiction throughout the entire Talmud. It sometimes took him more than four weeks to

---

1 Not all versions include the "intelligent heart" as a separate quality. Rashi is at a loss to understand the distinction between an understanding heart and an intelligent heart, and, indeed, *Midrash Shmuel* explains them as being one and the same attribute.

make sure that a *chiddush* "checked out" through all *Shas*. Only when his *chiddush* passed this test would Rav Abramsky publish it.

✦ ✦ ✦

✦ Rav Moshe Midner, one of the great scholars of Slonim, was very careful to examine any novel insights for halachic veracity before relating them to anyone else. He was once engaged in a deep discussion with a leading Rosh Yeshivah, who suggested an original line of reasoning to explain a statement of the Talmud. Rav Midner shuddered and asked, "Would you be willing to permit a woman to remarry based on that reasoning?"

The Rosh Yeshivah hesitated.

Rav Midner declared, "An insight that you would not rely on in practical halachah shows a lack of certainty as to its truth, and it should not be posited at all!"

✦ ✦ ✦

✦ Rav Moshe Feinstein was renowned for his volumes of halachic responsa, *Igros Moshe*. However, Reb Moshe also authored many volumes of *shiurim*, and a commentary on the Talmud entitled *Dibros Moshe*. It is reported that Reb Moshe once said he would accept the responsibility for halachic decisions that were based on any *sevara* he had written in *Dibros Moshe*. This was so because he would only publish a piece if he could stand by its defense (heard from Rav Shmuel Fuerst, *dayan* of Agudath Israel in Chicago).

The *Midrash Shmuel* adds that included in the attribute of an intelligent heart is the necessity to properly review the material one studies. It is not enough to quickly review the ideas superficially. Rather, one must carefully review the meaning of the concepts, too.

Others see in the attribute of intelligent heart a reference to studying the kabbalistic secrets of Torah. This is because one can only "peer" at the kabbalistic interpretations with one's heart; its knowledge is not a function of mental acuity alone, and it cannot be explained in the same manner as the revealed Torah (*Tiferes Yisrael*). In our times, our level of Torah learning, unfortunately, precludes a proper understanding of Kabbalah. It is even difficult to find a qualified *rebbi* for Kabbalah. However, just the knowledge that there exists a whole other dimension to Torah study and understanding increases one's appreciation of Torah and provides a stimulus to applying oneself with greater effort to learning Torah (*Cheshev HaEfod*).

Plan: ✦ *Analyze and review Torah thoughts carefully to ensure their halachic and logical veracity.*

6 AWE

אימה

We have explained earlier that Torah is not like any other field of knowledge — Torah is the word of Hashem. And so, Torah study cannot be approached in a lackadaisical manner. Torah must always be taken seriously and approached with awe and reverence. This awe is reflected in the focus one puts on Torah study, and the degree which one avoids any distractions from learning.

✦ The Chafetz Chaim once chastised his son, Reb Aryeh Leib, for speaking to a friend during his study session. Reb Aryeh Leib responded that it would not have been respectful to brush off a friend who had come to discuss something. The Chafetz Chaim disagreed. "Imagine a merchant who is busy serving his customers at the market," he said. "If an old friend approaches him in order to engage him in discussion, do you think he would stop and chat for a while? Of course not! After all, a person has to make a living. He would excuse himself and say that he is busy with his customers. He will ask whether the friend can come by to talk at another time.

"Torah study should be no different. If a person truly understands the importance of studying Torah, he will not waste any time in other discussion."

The way one studies Torah reflects the proper respect one must show. During davening, one may not touch any part of the body that is normally covered or scratch one's head, as it does not show proper respect. The same holds true while learning Torah. If one does touch or scratch a part of the body, at the very least it is necessary to rub one's hands on another surface (*Orach Chaim* 92:7; *Mishnah Berurah* 29).

✦ Rav Aharon Leib Steinman, *shlita*, sits on a bench rather than on a chair while studying Torah. He feels that leaning against the back of the chair does not show proper respect for the Torah. Instead, despite his advanced age, he sits almost rigidly, absorbed in study, yet cognizant that he is sitting before Hashem.

It is also important to show the proper respect for *sefarim*. For example, one should not place a *sefer* upside down (*Yoreh De'ah* 277:1). Nor should one leave a *sefer* open when he leaves the room (*Shach*, ibid.).

The qualities of respect and awe extend to all of the adjuncts of Torah learning. We have said earlier that, in order to acquire a proper understanding of Torah, one must study with a *rebbi* or teacher. A *rebbi* is more than just an educator; he represents a link in the chain of transmission of Torah from Sinai. As such, one must have the proper reverence and respect for him. The Mishnah in *Avos* (4:12) equates the reverence due a *rebbi* to that due to Hashem. The Maharal explains that without proper reverence, a person will not accept the *rebbi*'s teachings as the word of Hashem, but rather as a subjective opinion with which he is entitled to disagree.

Similarly, the Talmud warns that a student should only

learn from a teacher who is similar to an angel of Hashem (*Mo'ed Katan* 17a). How can a mere mortal be compared to an angel? We can explain the comparison with another idea from the Talmud. The Sages teach that a student must study Torah with the awe and reverence the Jewish people felt when they received the Torah at Mount Sinai (*Berachos* 22a). This means that the role of the *rebbi* is to bring the Sinai experience to his pupil. It is his task to impress upon his student the holiness and importance of Torah. His mission is, literally, like that of an angel, a Divine messenger, and he must be revered as such.

✦ Rabbi Akiva Eiger's reverence for the earlier commentators is evident throughout his writings. In a responsa to his son, he writes, "I am but dust under the feet of the Rashba, and I have not merited to understand his holy opinion [on this matter]." Similarly, he writes, "I fervently pray that Hashem illuminate my eyes and allow me to understand the words of our master [the Rashba]." Rabbi Akiva Eiger's awe for the *Rishonim* would not allow him to take issue with the Rashba; rather, he felt that he himself had to strive harder to understand his words.

✦ ✦ ✦

✦ Rav Chaim Volozhiner's son testified how his father's face would flush with awe and he would begin to tremble whenever he mentioned the words of his *rebbi*, the Gaon of Vilna. His reverence for his *rebbi* — even after the Gaon's death — was similar to how we imagine a mortal person would behave in the presence of an angel.

Plan: ✦ *Treat Torah study with appropriate respect, being vigilant about becoming distracted.*
✦ *Show the proper reverence for rebbeim.*

7 FEAR

יראה

Anyone who wishes to acquire Torah must also have the fear of sin (*Midrash Shmuel*). The Mishnah teaches that if one's fear of sin precedes his wisdom, his wisdom will endure. However, if one's wisdom precedes his fear of sin, his wisdom will not endure (*Avos* 3:9). There is a simple reason for this: If a person is concerned about sinning, he will be careful to listen attentively and make certain that each point in halachah is clarified, so that he will be able to observe it properly (*Tiferes Yisrael*).

◆ A person was once speaking with Rav Naftali Trop, Rosh Yeshivah of Radin. The man mentioned that some of the leading Roshei Yeshivah were blessed with phenomenal memories. Among the individuals mentioned was Rav Elchanan Wasserman. Reb Naftali disagreed. "Although it's true Reb Elchanan doesn't forget a thing he learns, I don't think he really has such an amazing memory. If you had Reb Elchanan's fear of Hashem, and his fear of forgetting even one word of Torah, you wouldn't forget a thing, either."

The Chazon Ish explains further: Unless a person has fear of Heaven, he will not merit the Divine assistance needed to properly understand the Torah, regardless of his level of intelligence. Even if such a person accomplishes something in his studies, it will not be the true Torah of Hashem (Rav Dov Yaffe, quoted in *Mishel HaAvos*).

✦ The Brisker Rav was once bothered by a very difficult Rashi. He challenged his students to offer a solution. No one could think of an explanation until one student, Rav Hillel Kagan, suggested a brilliant yet clear interpretation of the Rashi. The Rav was visibly impressed. "Oy, how much fear of Heaven is necessary to be able to think of such an answer!" he exclaimed.

✦ ✦ ✦

✦ The Klausenberger Rebbe, Rav Yekusiel Halberstam, once expressed a similar idea. "Yeshivah students sometimes think that if they study hard enough, they can become another Rashba. In truth, if someone wants to acquire the Torah of a Rashba, he must first learn how to acquire the *kedushah* of the Rashba, for only with the Rashba's fear of Heaven could one merit the Torah of the Rashba."

The Talmud says that a person who studies Torah without fear of Hashem can be compared to a watchman to whom the inner keys are entrusted, but not the outer keys (*Shabbos* 31b). Without the outer keys, the inner ones are useless. It is significant that both Torah study and the fear of Hashem are compared to keys, as they are both tools needed to enter into a relationship with Hashem. Fear of Hashem, however, is the primary tool — without it, Torah study will not accomplish anything.

The study of *mussar*, books of ethical refinement, helps a

person develop the fear of Hashem. *Mussar* reminds us of man's responsibilities to Hashem and the punishment that awaits us if we do not observe the Torah. The *Mishnah Berurah* (1:12) rules that there is an obligation to set aside a time each day to study *mussar*. Rav Itzele Peterberger (*Sha'arei Orah*, ch. 5–6) cites other sources, as well, that advocate learning *mussar* daily. The *Chayei Adam* (143) rules that one must learn *mussar* even at the expense of learning other parts of Torah, because the fear of Hashem is what Hashem wants from us more than anything else. As it says in *Avos*, "Without fear of Hashem, there can be no wisdom" (3:21).

✦ The Chasam Sofer would learn with his students from the *sefer Chovos HaLevavos* (Duties of the Heart) for fifteen minutes each day before beginning his *shiur*. He would tell his students, "Wisdom must begin with the fear of Hashem" (*Tehillim* 111:10).

Plan: ✦ *Learn some mussar each day to help develop fear of Heaven.*
✦ *Make an extra effort to clearly understand Torah learning and to commit it to memory.*

8 HUMILITY

ענוה

Humility is perhaps the most important trait for acquiring Torah. Moshe Rabbeinu received the Torah only because of his humility (*Midrash Shmuel*; Maharal). A person who is arrogant may be unwilling to seek assistance from others, and so will be inhibited to ask for help in his Torah study and spiritual growth. However, a humble person is not embarrassed to search out the truth, even if this means turning to a younger or seemingly less qualified person for answers to questions or to clarify his understanding. The Talmud teaches that a wise person is one who is willing to learn from everyone (*Avos* 4:1).

Humility is also the requisite for admitting when one is wrong. The Talmud says that erring is is a prerequisite for success (*Gittin* 43a). A person who cannot concede that he is wrong cannot learn from his mistakes and will not succeed.

⬥ Rav Shach was delivering a *shiur* when a young sixteen-year- old student posed a question from a *Tosafos*. Rav Shach thought for a few moments, then he closed his

Gemara and said, "You are correct; I must retract from what I said and I apologize for the mistake." Later, the Rosh Yeshivah added, "Actually, I did think of an answer that would have refuted the student's question, but it would not have been the correct understanding of *Tosafos*." And with that Rav Shach left the *beis midrash*.

◆When Rav Shlomo Zalman Auerbach applied for the position of Rosh Yeshivah at Yeshivas Kol Torah, he was invited to deliver a *shiur* before the yeshivah's staff. Shortly after beginning the *shiur*, one of the other Roshei Yeshivah, Rav Yona Merzbuch, challenged Reb Shlomo Zalman on a point he had made. Reb Shlomo Zalman conceded that he was in error. Somewhat embarrassed at having made such an error, Reb Shlomo Zalman was surprised when he was offered the job. Rav Merzbuch later explained that when the staff saw that this great scholar could so easily admit he was wrong, they knew he was the perfect person for the job.

On a spiritual level, Torah can only thrive in a modest person. The more a person is filled with feelings of self-importance, the less room there is, so to speak, for Torah. Thus we find that Moshe, who was the most humble of men (*Bemidbar* 12:3), received the Torah in a greater measure than any other person (*Ruach Chaim* 1:1).

The Talmud compares the Torah to water: Just as water travels from higher places to lower places, Torah leaves the arrogant person and resides in those who humble themselves (*Ta'anis* 7a). Regarding an arrogant person, we are taught that even if he is a scholar, his knowledge will be lost (*Pesachim* 66b).

◆ In the generation following the Vilna Gaon's passing, Rabbi Akiva Eiger and Rav Moshe Sofer, the Chasam

Sofer, were considered among the greatest Torah luminaries of their day. Their humility was also legendary. The Chasam Sofer, in fact, commented that Rabbi Akiva Eiger's humility paralleled that of Moshe Rabbeinu, to some extent. After the passing of the Chasam Sofer's first wife, the daughter of Rabbi Akiva Eiger was suggested to him as a match. Rabbi Akiva Eiger wrote a letter in which he expressed his amazement that Reb Moshe, whose level of piety and scholarship was "a thousand times greater than his own," would even consider the daughter of someone so undeserving. The Chasam Sofer responded that, to the contrary, he felt totally undeserving to marry into such a distinguished family.

Plan: ✦ *Have the courage to ask when something is not understood, and have the courage to admit mistakes.*
✦ *Try to avoid public honor.*
✦ *Recognize faults and behave with humility.*

9 JOY

שמחה

Joy is an outgrowth of love. One who loves the Torah will learn it with enthusiasm and joy. On the other hand, when one studies Torah without any pleasure, the learning is burdensome and will ultimately be forsaken (*Midrash Shmuel*). The Midrash actually says that if one relates words of Torah that are not as sweet as milk and honey to the listener, he is better off not saying them at all (*Shir HaShirim Rabbah* 4:23).

✦ Rav Moshe Shmuel Shapiro, *zt"l,* Rosh Yeshivah of Be'er Yaakov, related that he was once walking in Jerusalem on a cold snowy day, when he saw a figure in the distance jumping up and down. As he came closer he saw that this was none other than Rav Shach. Rav Shach explained that he had just left the Brisker Rav, who had shared with him a new insight regarding a difficult Rambam. Rav Shach had so much pleasure from the interpretation that he could not help but dance out of sheer joy.

✦ ✦ ✦

✦ Rav Eliezer Gordon, the Rav of Telz, was renowned for
his love of Torah. Once, two businessmen came to the
city of Telz to ask the Rav to adjudicate a dispute. Reb
Leizer, as he was called, excused himself, saying he was too
involved in a community matter and could not decide their
case at that time. The men decided to wait for the Rav.
Meanwhile, a yeshivah student came to the Rav and posed
a question on the *gemara* he was studying. Reb Leizer immediately turned his attention to the student, much to the
chagrin of the businessmen. When the Rav saw their distress, he explained. "You are right, I should not have answered the student either. But, what can I do? When it comes to Torah I am like an alcoholic who can't restrain himself. Torah discussion is my greatest pleasure in life!"

✦ ✦ ✦

✦ The Chazon Ish held Rav Shmuel Rozovsky, the Rosh
Yeshivah of Ponovezh, in high esteem. He once said
that Rav Shmuel was the generation's greatest Rosh
Yeshivah — a position he merited through the exceptional
joy and enthusiasm he showed when learning Torah.

Joy in learning Torah is also conducive to remembering Torah. The greater the joy one experiences, the better he will remember what he has learned (*Birkas Peretz*). A person can learn
more in one hour with joy than he can in several hours without
joy (*Ruach Chaim*).

✦ The Chafetz Chaim related that he had once heard an
old man describing the kaiser's visit to his town. The
visit had taken place more than seventy years earlier, when
the old man had been a young boy. The excitement of seeing the kaiser was such, that every detail of the visit —
from the color and shape of the coachman's hat to the

kaiser's elegant horse and wagon — were clearly etched in his memory. The Chafetz Chaim added that were a person to bring that same exuberance to studying Torah, he would remember every detail of his learning, too.

Several suggestions are offered concerning how one may achieve joy in Torah study. For example, *Sefer Chassidim* (158) states that singing a favorite tune brings joy to one's heart. This may also apply to learning Torah with a tune (*Midrash Shmuel*). Similarly, the human soul appreciates that which is aesthetically pleasing. Learning from a *sefer* that has clear print, fine paper, and a beautiful cover may create the high spirits and readiness of mind that enhance the joy of learning (preface to *Teshuvos Rav Akiva Eiger*).

> *Plan:* ✦ *Think about and appreciate the goodness constantly experienced and other joy-inducing thoughts.*
> ✦ *Sing the words of Torah while learning, and develop other strategies for increasing joy and appreciation while learning Torah.*

9a PURITY

טהרה

It almost goes without saying that one should purify his thoughts before studying Torah. We must focus on eliminating arrogant, lewd, hateful, and other such thoughts that the Torah condemns, before we learn. The pure and holy Torah cannot take root in a mind and heart that are steeped in impurity (*Midrash Shmuel*).

◆ Rav Yerucham Levovitz, the Mashgiach of Mir, was once in Vilna, where he saw the students from the university walking to their classes. He noted the spirit of levity and flirtatious behavior among the boys and girls attending the classes, and he saw that it affected neither their quest for knowledge nor their success in amassing that knowledge. He was struck by the contrast with Torah study. When it comes to Torah study, even subtly inappropriate behavior or remarks pose a major obstacle to learning, and thus to acquiring, Torah. The purity and holiness of the Torah precludes any type of behavior that is not consistent with a holy lifestyle.

The study of Torah also requires a pure relationship with one's body and purity in one's behavior.

✦ The Chazon Ish once tested a group of young boys on their Torah studies. At the conclusion of their discussion, the Chazon Ish indicated to the boys that he wanted to tell them something important. "Boys, be careful while learning Torah, that you never touch any part of your body that is normally covered. Doing so can interfere with your success in learning," he told them.

Similarly, the Chazon Ish would warn people to be meticulous about washing their hands properly in the morning, since purity of one's body is a necessary prerequisite to acquiring Torah.

Purity also means that one's learning should not be for ulterior motives, such as seeking honor. Torah study and the acquisition of knowledge should be solely for the fulfillment of Hashem's will and desire (*Mesillas Yesharim*, ch. 16).

It is not only learning Torah that requires purity; the preparations for teaching Torah also require purity in action and intention. An example of this can be seen in the Talmud (*Kesubos* 103b), where Rav Chiya relates how he would ensure that Torah not be forgotten. First he would grow cotton, from which he would make nets for ensnaring deer. He would then slaughter the deer; its flesh would be distributed among the poor, while the hide would be made into parchment. He would then transcribe the Torah on the parchment and teach it to several students. The students would, in turn, teach it to others. Thus Rav Chiya would ensure the transmission of Torah to the next generation.

The Maharsha asks, Why would Rav Chiya go to so much effort to procure parchment? Why did he not simply purchase it? He answers that Rav Chiya wanted to ensure that every step in the building of Torah would be done with the proper intentions. Only by supervising every single step — from growing the cotton, to making the nets, to producing the parchment — could

Rav Chiya guarantee that no improper thought mar the teaching and spreading of the Torah.

✦ Rav Elchanan Wasserman once visited the home of a wealthy family to seek funding for his yeshivah. There, he found the host playing cards with a group of friends. One of the players suggested that they donate the winnings to Reb Elchanan's yeshivah. Reb Elchanan refused the offer. "I'm sorry," he said, "but I cannot accept your offer. Torah can only be built with kosher money, and this money is not kosher."

The Sefas Emes once remarked that if one sees a student of Torah who applies himself, yet does not see success in his studies, it may very well mean that he is being supported by money coming from an impure source.

Plan: ✦ *Maintain proper thoughts, trying not to view or reflect on that which is harmful to a Torah way of life.*

✦ *Be careful to observe the laws regarding the purity of the body and purity in business affairs.*

✦ *Wash hands upon arising and after touching the parts of the body that are normally covered.*

✦ *Try to learn Torah for the sake of the mitzvah and not for any personal gain.*

10 SERVING SCHOLARS

שימוש חכמים

I t is not enough to study Torah from books and from teachers. Torah must also be acquired by observing the ways in which Torah scholars incorporate Torah into their everyday lives. After years of rigorous study, a physican must still complete a residency program in which he receives hands-on training under the tutelage of senior doctors. The residency may better prepare the physician than all the years of classroom study. Similarly, the Talmud tells us that observing the Torah personality provides a greater education than does years of Torah study (*Berachos* 7b). In fact, the Talmud states that one who has not served Torah scholars, even if he has studied Torah and Mishnah, is an ignoramus (*Berachos* 47b).

Rabbi Akiva described how he learned the importance of serving Torah scholars. He once found an unattended corpse on the road. He carried it more than four mil (a Talmudic measure) to the cemetery. When Rabbi Akiva related the incident to his teachers, they reprimanded him. Each step he had taken while carrying the body was tantamount to murder, they told him, since he had disgraced the corpse by not burying it in the place it was found. Rabbi Akiva concluded, "If, when I had good intentions, I incurred guilt, how much more so when my intentions were not good! From that moment on, I did not stop attending and assisting my teachers" (*Yerushalmi, Nazir* 7:1).

◆ Rav Elchanan Wasserman was one of the Chafetz Chaim's closest students. Many people would come to the Chafetz Chaim for advice or to discuss an issue, and, if the matter was not private, Reb Elchanan would ask them afterwards for a detailed account of the conversation. He would listen carefully to every nuance and detail. He explained that the Chafetz Chaim was like a Torah scroll, and his every word demanded attention. Reb Elchanan would also gaze intently at the Chafetz Chaim's countenance while listening to him speak.

One should observe one's *rebbi* in order to learn from his mundane behavior, as well as from his scholarship. Torah should not only affect our ritual practice; it should enter every area of our lives and influence all of our interactions with others. Thus, it is essential to witness, firsthand, those we need to emulate (*Lechem Shamayim*). A true *talmid* absorbs not only the wisdom of his *rebbi*, but also his outlook — and even his mannerisms.

◆ Rav Chaim Shmulevitz ran into a friend he had not seen since they had learned in Mir Yeshivah many years earlier. Reb Chaim began sharing some of his Torah insights with his friend and noticed him closing his eyes. Assuming that the man might be tired, Reb Chaim suggested they continue the discussion at another time. "No, please continue," the friend encouraged. "When I close my eyes and listen to you speak it's as if I hear our *rebbi*, Reb Yerucham, speaking!" Reb Chaim remarked that his friend's words gave him his greatest pleasure, for he now knew he had achieved the status of a real *talmid*.

Plan: ✦ *Make an effort to carefully observe the conduct of Torah scholars, in both their religious and mundane pursuits, and learn from their behavior.*

11 ATTENTIVENESS TO FRIENDS

דקדוק חברים

Torah cannot be acquired in a vacuum. A person who studies by himself will likely miss certain nuances and implications of the text. Moreover, the essence of Torah can only be acquired by two people learning together (*Derech Chaim*). The traditional means of learning with a *chavrusa*, or study partner, allows each person to be challenged and stimulated, resulting in a much fuller and deeper appreciation of the topic being studied. The Chazon Ish writes that a person studying alone cannot achieve even half of what is gained learning with a partner (*Kovetz Igros*).

◆ Rav Rafael Halperin, author of *Oneg Yom Tov*, was concentrating on his studies, when he suddenly stood up, walked to the window, and motioned to a passerby to come inside. When the man — a simple laborer — had entered the room, the Rav explained that he was unable to understand a difficult passage in the Talmud. He asked if the man would join him and see if they could figure it out together. The man, who had little Torah learning, was embarrassed. He asked the Rav what he could possibly contribute to the scholar's understanding. But the Rav insisted: "Two heads are better than one!" The Rav sat with the laborer and they studied the section together until the Rav finally worked out a solution.

The Talmud states that one learns more from a friend than from a teacher (*Ta'anis* 7a). This is because we do not stand in awe of a friend as we may with a *rebbi*; we are not as intimidated. We are more likely to challenge a friend's opinion in the pursuit of truth (*Lechem Shamayim*). Doing so sharpens the acumen of both students, and, ultimately, deepens their understanding.

⬥ Reish Lakish was Rav Yochanan's brother-in-law and *chavrusa*. When Reish Lakish passed away, Rav Yochanan was inconsolable. The Rabbis found him another *chavrusa*, an astute student named Rav Elazar ben Pedas. For every statement Rav Yochanan made, Rav Elazar cited many sources supporting Rav Yochanan's statement. Rav Yochanan became frustrated, lamenting Reish Lakish's loss. "Woe is to me," he cried, "Reish Lakish would challenge every statement I made with twenty-four questions, forcing me to defend my position in twenty-four different ways. That is the way to reach the truth. I don't need proofs to support me!" Eventually, Rav Yochanan became insane from grief, and the Rabbis prayed for his demise (*Bava Metzia* 84a).

Learning with a *chavrusa* may not come easily, as it carries potential risks — sparking feelings of jealousy, engendering the desire to win arguments, or providing the opportunity to socialize and become sidetracked into discussing other things. Nonetheless, the desire to succeed in Torah will enable the serious student to overcome these challenges (*Alei Shur*, p. 25).

Attentiveness to friends also means being careful with your choice of friends. Every person, no matter how virtuous, will be influenced by the company he keeps. Hashem even told our forefather Avraham to distance himself from Lot, lest he be influenced by his company. A person must surround himself with friends who share the common goal of growth in Torah and fear of Hashem.

> ✦ Rav Avraham Danzcig, author of *Chayei Adam*, recalled how, at the age of fourteen, before leaving his home to learn in yeshivah, his father made him take an oath that he would only befriend students who were serious in their service of Hashem. The seriousness of that oath remained seared in his mind, and served as an impetus to achieve such great success.

> *Plan:* ✦ *Find a chavrusa for Torah study who will be a good match.*
> ✦ *Be an active participant in the partnership, working towards clarifying the truth.*

12 Keen Discussion with Students
פלפול תלמידים

The Talmud states that one may learn more from his students than from his friends (*Ta'anis* 7a). Students tend to ask a greater number of questions than colleagues and friends, because they lack the experience and knowledge to discern whether or not a question is well-grounded or relevant. Furthermore, students may ask many questions to try to impress their *rebbi*. However, regardless of their intention, as a consequence of the questions, the *rebbi* must clarify, both for himself and for the student, why a question may or may not be valid. This process hones the intellect and enables both parties to arrive at the truth (*Lechem Shamayim*).

Working with the student also helps a *rebbi* with his own learning, because the *rebbi* is the pipeline through which Hashem's wisdom passes. As such, Hashem endows the *rebbi* with greater knowledge, so that he can pass it on to the students. Thus, both the *rebbi* and student gain (*Hafla'ah*).

In a fascinating statement, the Maharsha, in his commentary to *Sanhedrin* 42b, apologizes for not including his insights on that page of the Gemara. He explains that he had learned the page at the market fair, and he had been unable to discuss his insights with his students at the yeshivah. As a consequence, he felt his thoughts had not yet become sufficiently clarified, and were unworthy of publication.

Pilpul also refers to the methodology for learning Torah through which one questions, challenges, analyzes, and answers — building ideas upon principles and tearing down other ideas. Although it is important to develop a broad range of Torah knowledge, the primary understanding of Torah requires an in-depth give-and-take between teacher and student (*Levush Mordechai*, Foreword to *Bava Kama*).

✦ When Rav Eliezer Gordon, Rosh Yeshivah of Telshe, delivered his *shiur*, he would get no further than the first few words when he would be met by a barrage of questions, challenges, and comments from all sides of the room. Reb Leizer, as the Rosh Yeshivah was called, would excitedly join the foray, arguing with the students, enthusiastically defending his position, and cherishing every moment. The excitement would last for several minutes, until the Rosh Yeshivah continued to his next point. Then the room would explode with noise all over again. This dynamic repeated itself throughout the *shiur*. On one occasion, the students decided among themselves not to interrupt the Rosh Yeshivah, and to hold their questions until the conclusion of the *shiur*. Reb Leizer began to speak. He noticed the silence immediately. Cautiously, he continued to the next point. Again, not a sound was heard. Reb Leizer closed his Gemara and announced, "In a cemetery, Torah cannot be learned."

Plan: ✦ *Teach Torah to others and encourage them to ask questions on the material.*

13 COMPOSURE

ישוב

In order to understand Torah properly, it is necessary for a person to think in a calm, relaxed, and unhurried manner. It is very difficult to concentrate on learning when one feels pressured and under stress (*Derech Chaim*).

◆ In the Beis HaTalmud in Kelm, a major emphasis was placed on serving Hashem with *menuchas hanefesh*, calmness and tranquility. The *tefillos* were recited seriously and slowly, without any external show of exertion. Even *shuckling* (the traditional, forward and back swaying during prayer) was viewed as a form of impatience. During the learning *seder*, the students were disciplined to sit the entire time in their own seats and focus only on the volume in front of them. A fire once broke out near the yeshivah, and panic spread through the streets, as the houses all had flammable, thatched roofs. In the yeshivah, however, the study schedule continued as if nothing had happened.[1]

1 In describing this attribute of studying with composure, Rav Shlomo Wolbe related that he was once studying with his *chavrusa* in the Mir Yeshivah, when they saw another student running. "There must be a fire!" the *chavrusa* exclaimed. "How do you know?" Rav Wolbe asked. "It is inconceivable that a Mirrer student would be running like that for any

Torah learning must be done in an orderly and organized fashion to ensure a clear understanding of the subject (*Lechem Shamayim*).

Rav Elchanan Wasserman, Rosh Yeshivah of Baranovitch, explained the difference between the scholar who has an organized mind and one who does not: An organized mind can be compared to a library that has thousands of volumes neatly organized by topic. Such a library is a superb resource, since the information within is easily located. On the other hand, the scholar who is disorganized may be compared to a library whose books are poorly stored and sloppily indexed. Although this second library may have more books than the first one, it is an inadequate resource, because the books and information they hold is not accessible (heard from Rav Simcha Wasserman).

Being organized in one's general behavior makes it easier to focus on the intellectual and spiritual areas of life. Reb Simcha Zissel of Kelm would say that a person's external behavior reflects his inner person. If we see a person whose belongings are in disarray, we can assume that person's thinking is also disorganized. Similarly, if one is not careful about personal appearance and grooming, he is generally not careful with his spiritual appearance as well (*Tenuos HaMussar*).

◆ Rav Simcha Zissel Ziv, the Alter of Kelm, once visited his son, Reb Nochum Zev, who was attending yeshivah in Eishishok. Upon arriving at the yeshivah, the first thing Reb Simcha Zissel did was to check his son's lodgings, to see if his belongings were kept in a neat and orderly fashion. Finding that this was so, Reb Simcha Zissel said he was confident that his son was doing well in his studies.

To be able to concentrate, it is important to develop good

other reason," the young man replied.

study habits. The Meiri explains the Talmud's advice to designate a specific place for prayer along these lines (*Berachos* 6b): one's environment must be conducive to concentrating, he says. When a person prays consistently in the same place, distractions are minimized, allowing for better concentration. In fact, before sitting down to learn, one should always remove any object that distracts one's attention. One should also try to focus on only one thing at a time. The Chafetz Chaim advised that one should not allow a novel insight to be spoiled by another intruding idea (cited in *Mishel HaAvos*).

Midrash Shmuel adds that when one is asked a question, it is imperative to listen carefully and deliberately before answering, rather than responding hurriedly. *Shevus Yaakov* warns those who *pasken* not to issue a ruling without first checking the appropriate sources.

> *Plan:* ✦ *Prepare to learn Torah in a calm and orderly manner.*
> ✦ *Improve concentration by developing good study habits.*
> ✦ *Answer questions only after thinking them through carefully.*

14 KNOWLEDGE OF SCRIPTURES AND MISHNAH

מקרא ומשנה

A sound understanding of both *Tanach* and Mishnah is necessary for the acquisition of greatness in Torah, since those represent the foundation upon which the building can be built (*Midrash Shmuel*). Whereas *Tanach* is the foundation of the Written Law, Mishnah is the foundation of the Oral Law[1] (*Cheshev HaEfod*). One who tries to learn Talmud without a familiarity of *Tanach* and Mishnah will be deficient in ability and knowledge, because he lacks the foundation (Rav Yerucham Levovitz). Although one's primary curriculum should be Talmud, not *Tanach* (see *Rashi* on *Berachos* 28b), it is

---

1   The Mishnah (*Avos* 5:21) thus says that a child should master *Tanach* during the period of five to ten years of age; Mishnah should be mastered at ten to fifteen years of age. Only after both these tasks have been accomplished should the student begin studying Talmud.

nonetheless assumed that one is already fluent in Tanach.

> ✦ The Chafetz Chaim always carried a little volume of
> *Tanach* in his tallis bag. He would learn from it each
> day, until he had mastered all *Tanach* by heart. He con-
> stantly encouraged his students to learn the entire weekly
> Torah portion with Rashi. He told them it was not suffi-
> cient to merely review the portion *shnayim mikra v'echad*
> *targum* since we do not really understand *Targum*, and
> Rashi offers us the clearest explanation of the Torah.

Rashi (on *Shemos* 31:18) quotes a Midrash in which the Torah is compared to a bride. Just as a bride adorns herself with
twenty-four pieces of jewelry (*Yeshayah* 3:18-22), a scholar must
be fluent in the twenty-four books of *Tanach*. A scholar should
also be proficient in the six orders of Mishnah. *Shulchan Aruch*
HaRav (*Talmud Torah*, ch. 2) suggests that "Mishnah" refers to
learning halachic rulings without delving into their reasoning,
as opposed to studying Gemara. Studying "Mishnah" would
thus also include studying *Shulchan Aruch* and other halachic
sefarim.

Many *sefarim* recommend memorizing *mishnayos*. This
enables a person to occupy his mind with Torah at all times,
even when he has no access to a *sefer*. In fact, Rav Yosef Karo, the
Beis Yosef, merited learning Torah from a *malach*, an angel, only
because of his proficiency in Mishnah (*Maggid Meisharim*).

> ✦ Rav Mordechai Gifter, the Telzer Rosh Yeshivah, de-
> scribed his first visit to the Steipler Gaon. The Steipler
> was so very hard of hearing that people generally commu-
> nicated with him by writing him notes. The Gaon would
> then respond vocally. Rav Gifter noticed that while he was
> writing down his words, the Gaon seemed to be mumbling
> to himself. He learned afterwards that the Steipler always

recited *mishnayos* from memory while his visitors put pen to paper, so as not to lose a moment that could be spent learning Torah.

✦ ✦ ✦

✦ The great *posek* Rav Moshe Feinstein spent every spare moment learning *mishnayos* by heart. During the Torah reading, Rav Moshe would study *mishnayos* until the first *oleh* recited the opening *berachah*. Then he would rush to the *bimah* and listen to the *leining*. At the conclusion of the *aliyah*, he would rush back to his seat and resume his study until the next *berachah*.

Plan: ✦ *Set up a regular session to study and review Tanach and Mishnah, perhaps for a few minutes each day.*

15 MINIMAL SLEEP

מיעוט שינה

Although sleep is a human necessity, too much sleep can be a major hindrance to the acquisition of Torah. Sleep is a physical, and sometimes emotional, need. But the more a person is attentive to his physical nature, the more he is separated from the spiritual and intellectual world (*Derech Chaim*). Furthermore, too much sleep causes a person to become intellectually sluggish (*Tiferes Yisrael*). Thus, one who sleeps too much cannot succeed in achieving greatness in Torah study.

✦ Rabbi Berel Wein relates how, as a rabbi in Miami Beach, he had the opportunity to chauffeur the Ponovezher Rav for a fundraising mission for his yeshivah. After several hours of meetings, Rabbi Wein, who was the Rav's junior by several decades, was tired and suggested they take a break so the Rav could rest a bit. The Ponovezher Rav smiled and responded, "Look, I'm already an old man. Soon I will have all the time in the world to rest and sleep. As long as I am here, though, I must work as hard as I can. There's no time for me to sleep now!"

The Rambam (*Hilchos Dei'os* 4:8) advises that a person sleep eight hours a night. The Chazon Ish warned students not to sleep less than seven hours, but he added that the hours could be spread throughout the day, for example, six at night and one during the day (*Ma'asei Ish*). The *Tiferes Yisrael* notes that as one ages, he needs less sleep. For an older person, five or six hours may suffice.

✦ Rav Elchanan Wasserman instructed his students to sleep properly, although he slept very little himself. (Apparently, he knew how much sleep he needed for his own strength.) Each night he walked from his home to the yeshivah at around midnight, in order to turn out the lights and to encourage the students to go to sleep. He would gently remind them that there is a time to study Torah and there is a time to sleep. He felt that staying up late, even to learn, was the work of the *yetzer hara*. Although in the short term, a person may appear to gain by cutting back on sleep, ultimately, he will lose more than he gains, and his learning will suffer.

That being said, however, there is an opinion in the Talmud (*Eiruvin* 65a) that night was created for the purpose of Torah study; thus, one should dedicate at least part of the night to study (see *Mishnah Berurah* 238:1).

✦ Rav Aryeh Leib Grossnass came to Radin, Poland from Germany, as a young boy of fourteen. The Rosh Yeshivah, Rav Naftali Trop, asked him why he had left Germany to learn in Radin. Aryeh Leib answered, "At the yeshivah in Germany they only study Torah by day, but here they study both by day and by night." The answer pleased Reb Naftali, and the young man was accepted as a student.

Plan: ✦ *Make sure to have sufficient sleep, while not sleeping any longer than necessary, and devote the extra time to studying Torah.*

16 MINIMAL CONVERSATION

מיעוט שיחה

The power of speech is one of Hashem's greatest gifts to man. As such, it is important that this gift not be squandered. The Talmud teaches that thoughtless chatter is forbidden, especially if it takes time away from Torah study (*Yoma* 19b). The Torah says, "You shall speak *in them*" (*Devarim* 6:7), which means that "you shall speak in words of Torah, not in words of empty talk." The gift of speech was intended to be used for constructive purposes, such as learning Torah. Its misuse wastes opportunities for growth in Torah.

◆ The Chafetz Chaim once traveled with his son-in-law, Reb Tzvi, to Moscow to meet with a wealthy benefactor. While the Chafetz Chaim was speaking with the potential donor, Reb Tzvi was in the next room composing the text of a telegram. In the course of conversation, the discussion veered towards *lashon hara*. The Chafetz Chaim pointed to his son-in-law and said to the man, "See how carefully a person writes a telegram: writing words, crossing them out, and replacing them. Each word costs money and must be carefully considered. That's how careful we have to be with each word that comes from our mouths!"

Interrupting one's study with empty talk shows disrespect and lack of appreciation for the importance of Torah. Success in Torah requires consistent learning, with no interruptions. Regarding Torah study, Rav Yosef Leib Bloch said that 12+12 does not equal 24.[1] He meant that an hour of learning and another separate hour of learning, cannot be compared to the cumulative effect that results from two consecutive hours of learning. (Rav Chaim Shmulevitz made a similar observation, see *The Rosh Yeshivah*, p. 135.)

♦ Rav Elchanan Wasserman was deeply engrossed in a Torah discussion with his *chavrusa*, when a messenger entered the room to inform him that his wife, who was in a different town, had just delivered a baby. Reb Elchanan stood up, said *"mazel tov!"* recited the appropriate *berachah*, and then immediately returned to the discussion with his *chavrusa*.

Unnecessary speech should be avoided, even when speaking constructively. The Torah is very precise in its own wording, often leaving major halachos to be learned from an extra word, or even a single letter. The Talmud similarly instructs the teacher to teach his students in as clear and concise a manner as possible (*Chullin* 63b).

1 This comment was made regarding Rabbi Akiva, who upon returning home after twelve years of study overheard his wife say she would allow him to return for another twelve years. Rabbi Akiva immediately returned for another twelve years, without even entering his home. Rav Bloch explained that had Rabbi Akiva stopped in to visit, his accomplishment would not have been the same.

Rav Yaakov Kaminetzky cites the Vilna Gaon, who was of the opinion that every word of Torah studied is a new mitzvah. Reb Yaakov qualifies this statement, explaining that this only applies when the words studied are those of an author who is precise in his language. It is illogical to assume that a person receives reward for studying an author's redundant wording, merely because the author could not express himself clearly in fewer words (*Emes L'Yaakov*).

✦ Someone once asked Rav Chaim Brisker why his responses were always so terse. Reb Chaim answered with a parable. A man was trying to find his way out of a pitch dark house. If he is the owner and is very familiar with the layout of the house, he will find his way out quickly and easily. If he is a newcomer to the house, however, he will have to feel his way around the walls, stumbling in the dark, before he is able to find the exit. Similarly, one who knows and understands the material can explain it clearly and concisely. If a person must offer a lengthy explanation, it signifies a lack of clarity.

✦ ✦ ✦

✦ Rav Pesach Stein, Rosh Yeshivah in Telshe-Cleveland, was renowned for his *shiurim*, and for his ability to clarify profound concepts clearly and concisely. He used to say that he put more effort into deciding what not to say than in deciding what to say.

Plan: ✦ *Avoid idle speech, especially during Torah study. Try to be clear and concise when explaining Torah.*

16 a MINIMAL BUSINESS

מיעוט סחורה

Hashem created the world in such a manner that human beings must support themselves and their families. Yet, as with other human endeavors, involvement in business or a profession carries many spiritual risks. On one hand, work can actually assist one's spiritual growth. We learn in *Avos* (2:5) that Torah study that is not accompanied by work cannot thrive. On the other hand, work is necessarily time-consuming, and, for some, may also be addictive. The nature of work is that it allows little time for other pursuits — most importantly, Torah study. That is why the Talmud states that Torah cannot be found among business entrepreneurs or merchants (*Eiruvin* 55a). A person whose mind is constantly drawn to new opportunities for making money can hardly concentrate on Torah. The only way to avoid this pitfall is to keep one's involvement in earning a living to a minimum (*Midrash Shmuel*).

✦ The great *posek*, Rav Shlomo Zalman Auerbach, was given a piece of land in Bat Yam as a dowry. Shortly after his wedding, rumor had it that the British government was planning to impose a new tax on empty lots, and people were trying to figure out ways to avoid paying the high tax. Reb Shlomo Zalman sensed that these financial concerns were interfering with his learning. So he went to Bat Yam, walked into the first real estate office he came across, and put his lot up for sale. It was sold to the first customer who made an offer, although the offer was well below the market value of the property. Reb Shlomo Zalman returned to Jerusalem, happy that he could now learn without distraction.

Becoming too absorbed in one's job also belies a lack of trust in Hashem. The Talmud states that a person's livelihood is decided on Rosh HaShanah (*Beitzah* 16a). How much or how little effort one puts into his work has no effect on his income. We must trust that if we fulfill His will and delve into His Torah, Hashem will not allow us to suffer from want.

The *Chovos HaLevavos* relates an incident regarding a righteous person who journeyed overseas to seek his livelihood. During his travels he met an idol worshipper. The righteous man mocked the heathen's belief in a god who was powerless to help, whereupon the heathen asked about the righteous man's belief. "I believe in the Creator who sustains the whole world," the man replied. "Your actions belie your words," the heathen challenged. "If you really believe your G-d sustains the whole world, why did you travel so far to eke out a livelihood? Couldn't G-d sustain you in your hometown as easily as He could support you here?" The righteous man realized his companion was right and traveled home.

The Chafetz Chaim says that a person who is serious about

Torah study, and who uses any time available for studying Torah, will be rewarded even for the time he spends working. The person's actions prove that, had it been possible, the time would have been used for learning. But when one squanders his spare time, he is taken to task even for the time he spends working, since he has shown that had he not worked, he would not have studied in any case. For a person whose primary concern is Torah learning, work need not be considered an interruption.

✦ Rav Shlomo Eiger, besides being a great scholar, was also a successful merchant. Often, he would be called away from his studies for several hours at a time for some pressing business matter. As soon as he returned, however, he would continue his study and resume his discussion from the exact place he had left off. He related that his father, the great Rabbi Akiva Eiger, had blessed him at his wedding that he never become so involved in his business dealings that he had to search to remember where he had left off learning.

Plan: ✦ *Reduce daily work concerns in order to have more time for concentrating on Torah study.*

17 MINIMAL PLEASURE

מיעוט תענוג

Physical pleasure is Hashem's gift to humankind so that we feel content, joyous, and relaxed. These feelings help us to be loving beings, and enable us to appreciate Hashem and His handiwork. They also help create an expansive state of mind, which is beneficial to Torah study.

However, indulging in excess pleasure presents problems similar to those discussed above regarding conversation, sleep, and work. Too much pleasure can jeopardize a person's connection to Torah. In fact, the Torah itself warns about the dangers of excess pleasure with the words "Yeshurun waxed fat and kicked" (*Devarim* 32:15). The Seforno explains this to mean that when the elite of the nation pursue excessive physical pleasure, it leads to desertion of Hashem. *Tanna D'vei Eliyahu Rabbah* (26) couches this idea in practical terms: Before a person prays that Torah enter his being, he should first pray that delicacies not enter his belly (*Midrash Shmuel; Lechem Shamayim*).

◆ Not long after Rav Yosef Chaim Sonnenfeld, the Rav of Yerushalayim, married his second wife, she served him a bowl of delicious soup. Reb Yosef Chaim tasted some of the soup and left the rest in the bowl. When his wife re-entered the room, he first praised her culinary talents and then apologized, saying, "Delicacies like this during the week are a little too much for me. All my life I have been careful not to pamper my body and to be satisfied with only what is necessary. Now, in my old age, why should I ruin what I've worked so hard to accomplish? Please save this type of food for Shabbos when I will be more than happy to enjoy it."

The Maharal explains that one who pursues physical pleasure shows that he identifies with the physical and material world. That identification makes it difficult for him to absorb Torah wisdom, which represents an identity with the inner, spiritual world (*Derech Chaim*). The more one distances himself from the physical, the more he is able to appreciate the spiritual. The Talmud states that the words of Torah only remain with someone who "dies" over Torah, which can be understood as sacrificing one's physical desires for the sake of Torah (*Berachos* 43b).

◆ The Netziv, Rav Naftali Tzvi Yehudah Berlin, once visited the Rashash, Rav Shmuel Strashen. The Rashash asked his guest about a *Tosafos* he found difficult to understand. The Netziv thought for a few moments and then clarified the *Tosafos*.[1] The Rashash was amazed that the Netziv seemed to work out the explanation so easily, when, after so much effort he still could not understand it. The Netziv explained, "Reb Shmuel, you are a wealthy man, and you study in comfort. I, on the other hand, study

1   Cited in *Rashash* (*Yevamos* 81b).

in poverty and under difficult circumstances. When one studies under such challenges, he is privy to special Divine assistance...."

A person who consumes all types of delicacies can develop a habit of feeding deep, spiritual cravings with shallow, physical pleasures. This habit makes it much more difficult to appreciate the sweetness of the spiritual pleasure of Torah study.

✦ A relative of Rav Moshe Feinstein once visited him on a very hot day. Reb Moshe was absorbed in study and sweating profusely. The visitor observed an air conditioner in the window behind Reb Moshe's desk , but it wasn't turned on. Reb Moshe explained that he did not use the air conditioner because if he became accustomed to studying in comfort, he was afraid that he would be unable to learn if the air conditioner broke. So, he had decided never to learn with the air conditioner turned on.

Plan: ✦ *Limit physical pleasure.*
    ✦ *When experiencing physical pleasure, try to use it as a means of appreciating Hashem, and achieving spiritual gain.*
    ✦ *Avoid pleasure solely for self-gratification.*

18 MINIMAL LAUGHTER

מיעוט שחוק

Laughter is an emotional response elicited by an enjoyable situation, either beneficial or otherwise. The intense joy of studying Torah and performing mitzvos can elicit one type of laughter. That form of laughter shows a great appreciation and enjoyment of Torah, and is always encouraged.

Silliness and mockery produce a different kind of laughter. It is that type of raucous laughter that the Talmud warns leads to immoral behavior (*Avos* 3:13). *Mesillas Yesharim* (ch. 5) similarly decries the laughter of foolishness and mockery, comparing it to a shield smeared with oil that deflects words of inspiration or rebuke from making their way into one's heart. This, understandably, must always be avoided.

The laughter that should be reduced as a means for acquiring Torah is a different form of laughter — the laughter that comes from a sense of humor (*Cheshev HaEfod*). A good sense of humor can be very beneficial, as it can lift one's spirits and help create a pleasant environment. When used properly and under the right circumstances, a joke is meritorious. The Talmud relates that once, in the marketplace, Eliyahu HaNavi pointed out two ordinary people who were destined for *Olam HaBa*, simply because they would cheer up despondent people with their jokes and laughter (*Ta'anis* 22a). Similarly, Rabbah would begin teaching Torah with a witty comment (*Shabbos* 30b). Laughter relaxes people physically and mentally. When people feel more relaxed they are better able to study Torah and serve Hashem (*Midrash Shmuel*).

♦ Whenever the Beis Yisrael of Gur chastised one of his followers, he always concluded his criticism with a humorous comment. He explained that when a person needs to express anger, he should always employ humor to soften his words.

However, even good humor can interfere with one's growth in Torah. The Maharal (*Derech Chaim*) explains that laughter generally stems from the ironic or the ridiculous, both of which run counter to the logical paths of the intellect. Thus, too much humor can interfere with the intellectual pursuit of Torah study. Furthermore, laughter takes one's mind off other things, including Torah (*Rabbeinu Yonah* on *Rif*, *Berachos* 31a). While the Rabbis do recommend using a little humor, they do not recommend using more than that.

♦ Rav Elyah Dushnitzer, the Lomzer Mashgiach, was careful to control his laughter. Even when he saw something very funny, he would cover part of his mouth with his hand to cut short his laugh, in keeping with the Talmudic dictum that "one should not fill his mouth with mirth in this world" (*Berachos* 31a).

♦ ♦ ♦

✦ Rav Elchanan Wasserman was very measured in his laughter, avoiding conversations and situations that could cause him to laugh. When he was with someone who had made a witty comment, Reb Elchanan would smile, so as not to insult his companion, but he would not allow himself to laugh. In this he followed the ways of his *rebbi*, the Chafetz Chaim, who was also very disciplined regarding laughter. Yet, in those instances where he deemed it proper to laugh, such as poking fun at idolatry or heresy,[1] the Chafetz Chaim even asked others to relate funny stories. He would laugh heartily at them.

Plan: ✦ *Use humor principally to serve some constructive purpose.*

---

1 See *Megillah* 25b.

19 MINIMAL TIME SPENT ON WORLDLY MATTERS
מיעוט דרך ארץ

D*erech Eretz* has several meanings. Each of them has relevance to the acquisition of Torah. One definition of *derech eretz* is good character, or *menschlichkeit*. Regarding this, the Mishnah warns that without *derech eretz* there can be no Torah (*Avos* 3:17). A person must have good character before he can acquire Torah. Rav Shmuel Rozovsky comments that a person lacking sensitivity is incapable of understanding the subtleties of Torah analysis (*Mishel HaAvos*).

◆ An incident once occurred in the town of Mir, in Poland. The police confronted a group of students and asked for their identification papers. One student's papers were at his lodgings, so the police accompanied him to his room, while his friends returned to the yeshivah. The following day, Rav Yerucham Levovitz told the students he was considering closing the yeshivah. "How could students of Torah allow a friend to leave with the police unaccompanied? Who knows what they could have done to him? How could you be so insensitive to his fear? All your Torah is worthless if it is not accompanied by good character."

Another interpretation of *derech eretz* is proper etiquette. While etiquette is important, it may be necessary, at times, not to do what is socially expected, if it conflicts with halachah or one's Torah study schedule. Sometimes a person must put his own spiritual needs ahead of the needs of others.

◆ A young *kollel* student asked Rav Shlomo Zalman Auerbach if he should attend all his friends' weddings. Though he understood it is a great mitzvah to rejoice with a bride and groom, he was concerned he would have to attend *simchah*s every night, and as a result, his learning would suffer. Reb Shlomo Zalman responded, "When I attend *simchah*s, I can stop by for a few moments to wish *mazel tov*, and everyone appreciates my coming. When I was younger, however, I rarely went to weddings, because I had to study. Today they appreciate when I show my face for a few minutes, because previously I spent that time learning. Had I gone to all those weddings in my youth, who would even look at me today?"

Another interpretation of *derech eretz* is general worldliness. Some familiarity with languages, current events, business practices, and other such practical knowledge is beneficial for interpersonal relationships. However, one should not invest more time or effort than is necessary into this pursuit, as it can interfere with growth in Torah.

✦ I once asked a prominent Rosh Yeshivah if he felt it was important to keep abreast of the news. He told me he thought it was worthwhile listening to the headlines each morning, but not more than that, for this should be enough to familiarize oneself with the goings-on. But, he added, beware of news junkies, who spend hours listening to the same news over and over again, wasting time that could be used for Torah study.

Derech eretz is also a euphemism for the physical relationship between a husband and wife. The Torah student must be sensitive to his wife's needs, in order to be a supportive spouse and contribute to a peaceful home. At the same time, however, he must realize the necessity for moderation in this area. Overindulgence in the physical weakens a person's strength and ability to concentrate properly (*Tiferes Yisrael; Cheshev HaEfod*). Proper guidance from a mentor is necessary, of course, for finding the proper balance.

Plan: ✦ *Develop good character traits and be a mensch.*
✦ *Do not allow excessive politeness to interfere with growth.*
✦ *Limit worldly interests to what is important to know.*

20 PATIENCE

ארך אפים

Patience is necessary for both teacher and student of Torah. The Mishnah states that an impatient person cannot impart knowledge to his students (*Avos* 2:5). A teacher's impatience discourages his students from asking questions, and if students do not ask questions, their comprehension of the subject is reduced (*Ruach Chaim*). Rav Aharon Kotler elaborates that a lack of patience stems from a lack of love, and a teacher who does not love his students cannot inculcate them with Torah (*Mishnas Rav Aharon*). *Lechem Shamayim* adds that the Torah personality must learn to emulate Hashem's abundant patience.

✦ Rav Isser Zalman Meltzer, the Slutzker Rav, once tested a group of young students at the Eitz Chaim Yeshivah. One student explained a *Tosafos* incorrectly. Reb Isser Zalman corrected him, but the student insisted that his interpretation was right. Reb Isser Zalman explained it once more, and again the boy insisted he was right. Beginning to lose patience with the student, Reb Isser Zalman excused himself and went outside. He murmured to himself, "Remember — he is only a young student who must be taught. How can I lose my patience with him?" Then he returned to the room, and patiently began explaining the *Tosafos* again.

A student must also practice patience in order to be able to learn. Impatience prevents a person from investing the time and energy needed to understand the material properly.

The Talmud relates that Rav Preida had a student with slow comprehension. In fact, Rav Preida would teach him the material four hundred times before he would understand. Once, the student knew that Rav Preida had to leave and, feeling under pressure, he could not concentrate. Even after four hundred times, he still did not understand the material. Rav Preida assured the student he would not leave until he understood the lesson. He patiently repeated the lesson another four hundred times, until the student understood. Rav Preida was rewarded with longevity and his entire generation received a share in *Olam HaBa* in the merit of his unbelievable patience (*Eiruvin* 54b).

Impatience also often leads to anger, one of the most destructive human traits. Anger is generally counterproductive — it usually engenders tension, and often only serves to aggravate the situation. Perhaps worst of all, it causes a person to forget his learning (*Pesachim* 66b).

⬥ Rabbi Hillel Goldberg was a student of Rav Ben-Tzion Bruk, the Novardok Rosh Yeshivah. In all the years Rabbi Goldberg knew him, he saw Rav Bruk upset just once. After those few uncomfortable minutes, the Rosh Yeshivah asked Rabbi Goldberg to bring him a Gemara *Pesachim*. He took the volume and began searching through it, leafing back and forth, unsuccessfully. Finally, after a few minutes, he turned to his student and said, "You see, Reb Hillel? Somewhere in this volume it says that when one gets angry he forgets his wisdom. Here you have a clear fulfillment of that dictum, because I can't even find it!"

Plan: ✦ *Be patient in teaching others, as well as in one's own learning.*
  ✦ *Control anger.*

21 A Good Heart

לב טוב

aving a good heart refers to the quality of always wanting to help others (according to one's ability), and not feeling any malice or ill-will towards them (Rambam). Although this quality may seem unrelated to scholarship, Rav Meir Chodosh, Mashgiach of Chevron Yeshivah, explains that we should not think of helping others as an impediment to personal growth in Torah. Quite the contrary, from the Mishnah we learn that the existence of the world stands upon three pillars: Torah study; the service of Hashem (or prayer); and kind deeds (*Avos* 1:2). It is impossible to grow in Torah without both service and kindness (cited in *Mishel HaAvos*).

✦ A Torah scholar once approached the Chazon Ish with a problem. He was constantly being asked to involve himself in community projects, and he felt that community work was interfering with his time for Torah study. He wanted to know if he should free himself from the *chesed* projects he was involved in. The Chazon Ish responded that in order to acquire Torah, one must have a clarity of mind, and performing *chesed* actually contributes to one's clarity of mind.

In discussing the balance one should strike between performing acts of kindness and devoting oneself to Torah study, the Brisker Rav quoted his father Reb Chaim: One who closes his Gemara to do a *chesed*, is considered in Heaven as if his Gemara is still open. On the other hand, one who opens his Gemara to avoid doing a *chesed*, is considered as if his Gemara remains closed (*Toras Chaim, Kuntres Limud Torah*, p. 85).

Having a good heart includes rejoicing over another's success, and not feeling jealousy. Jealousy can consume the heart and mind and preclude concentrating on one's own goals (*Matnas Chaim*). One should not envy another's success in Torah, either.[1]

✦ Reb Shraga Feivel Mendlowitz, *menahel* of Mesivta Torah Vodaath, was the quintessential "good heart." When he heard that Rav Aharon Kotler was trying to start a yeshivah in Lakewood, New Jersey, he immediately spoke to several of the top students in his yeshivah and convinced them to follow Rav Aharon. When the other Roshei Yeshivah protested that the yeshivah was losing its core of top students, Reb Shraga Feivel responded that his sole concern was what was best for Hashem and for the Torah, and not what was best for Torah Vodaath. He did the

---

1 Although the Talmud (*Bava Basra* 21a) says that jealousy among scholars increases wisdom, implying that jealousy stimulates Torah study, the Maharsha (ibid.) explains that this only refers to children, who may need more mundane incentives to excel in their Torah study. Rav Shlomo Wolbe, in contrast, explains that the Talmud is referring to mature scholars, whose jealousy is not directed at individuals, but rather is an expression of a burning desire for greater knowledge. Most people are not capable of the type of jealousy that rises above the lower, subjective level of being directed against individuals (heard from Rav Wolbe).

same for Rav Elya Meir Bloch when he started the Telshe Yeshivah in Cleveland. He truly rejoiced over the success of other yeshivahs.

Having a good heart also means forgiving others and not bearing resentment (*Midrash Shmuel*).

✦ Rav Isser Zalman Meltzer had a serious disagreement with Rav Pesach Pruskin regarding a yeshivah they headed together. This dispute resulted in Reb Pesach wanting to leave to start his own yeshivah, taking a group of students with him. Reb Isser Zalman strongly opposed this proposal. They brought their dispute to Rav Dovid Feinstein (father of Rav Moshe Feinstein) to decide between them. Reb Dovid ruled that Reb Pesach could take only six students to start his yeshivah. Reb Pesach took six students and started a yeshivah in Shklov. At the dedication of the new yeshivah, Reb Isser Zalman was the guest of honor. Once the dispute had been settled, Reb Isser Zalman ceased to complain, and he never expressed any resentment toward Reb Pesach.

Plan: ✦ *Help others in any way possible, trying to remove any feelings of jealousy or resentment by thinking about their fine qualities.*

22 FAITH IN THE SAGES

אמונת חכמים

The Torah was given to the Sages to interpret, and it is their interpretation that defines Torah. It is for this reason that a person must have faith in the scholars of each generation, for without them a person could not understand even one word of Torah properly (*Lechem Shamayim*). Even if a person cannot fathom the Sages' words, he must realize the problem arises from *his* inability to understand — it does not lie with the Sages (*Ya'avetz*).

✦ The Steipler Gaon's family once noticed that he was distressed. He explained that the Chazon Ish had posed a question. The Steipler had responded that the Chasam Sofer discussed this question in his responsa. The Chazon Ish, however, had insisted there was no such responsa. Although the Steipler had seen the responsa himself, he felt that if the Chazon Ish had said that the Chasam Sofer had not said it, there was no alternative but to believe that this volume was a forgery. This caused the Steipler great distress.

The following day, the family saw the Steipler's face aglow. When asked about the change, the Steipler said that the Chazon Ish had admitted that he was mistaken: the Chasam Sofer did indeed discuss the question. Not for a moment had the Steipler even suspected the Chazon Ish might be wrong, and he was now overjoyed that the responsa of the Chasam Sofer that he had cited was indeed authentic.

Another reason why it is so important to turn to the Sages is for guidance in one's spiritual growth. Because the Sages have already learned to overcome life's challenges, they are in the unique position to be able to guide those who have not yet done so. The *Mesillas Yesharim* (ch. 3) compares life to a maze in which people try to find their way. Only the person who has already found his way to the middle of the maze is capable of directing others.

Rav Yitzchak Hutner writes that many people mistakenly think that *gedolei Yisrael* are born great and need not work very hard to develop their *middos*. Because it is difficult for the average person to identify with such purity of character, he believes that such a person is simply fashioned that way by Hashem. This misunderstanding diminishes the potential influence of the Sages, and the reality is quite different. The Chafetz Chaim, for example, endured many struggles to overcome the sin of *lashon hara* in his earlier years. He probably failed many times, too. But he persevered until, eventually, he became the Chafetz Chaim. Every person can learn from his example. By believing that greatness comes naturally and easily to those who demonstrate greatness, we may fail to work as hard as is necessary to achieve greatness ourselves (*Igros* 128).

Faith in the Sages does not preclude asking questions. But the student must be willing to accept his *rebbi's* reasoning, even if he does not understand it or agree with it. If, however, one thinks he can gauge the correctness of the *rebbi's* opinion through his own understanding, he is derelict in his faith (*Michtav MeEliyahu*).

One should not refrain from asking Torah leaders questions out of the concern that "they won't understand where I'm coming from." The Talmud (*Sanhedrin* 110a) warns that one who doubts his *rebbi* is considered to have doubted the Shechinah (*Alei Shur*).

It is also important to verify what the *gedolei Yisrael* really believe, as their words and opinions are often distorted. Anecdotal evidence must also be clarified, as a seemingly minor distinction in a situation may result in a totally different ruling. Accepting unconfirmed stories about Torah leaders can actually harm one's faith in the Sages (*Alei Shur*).

> ✦ The Chazon Ish used to say, "Whatever they say over in my name is false! And if it's not absolutely false, it's half-false!" Rav Moshe Feinstein commented similarly, "I don't mind when people repeat my opinions and rulings in their own names. I'm more concerned when they repeat their opinions in my name!"

Plan: ✦ *Seek the advice and guidance of Torah scholars. Accept it even if it is hard to understand.*

23 ACCEPTING SUFFERING

קבלת יסורים

Human suffering, especially that of the righteous, has always been a mystery to humankind. We feel that we cannot fathom the ways of Hashem. The Talmud, however, does provide some general guidance and insight into the purpose of suffering (*Berachos* 5b). One reason for suffering is in order to increase a person's reward; one receives more reward for overcoming challenges. Torah study, specifically, can only be acquired through suffering (ibid. 5a). This means that in order to integrate the Torah into one's very being, one must persevere and study it under trying circumstances. Ideally, a student's love and devotion to Torah should be so deep that he does not allow suffering to interfere with his study. One should actually strengthen his bond to Torah during a period of suffering.

✦ Rav Chaim Shmulevitz, the Mirrer Rosh Yeshivah, suffered from terrible, chronic pain in his later years, yet he once told his *chavrusa* that in twenty-four years he only missed delivering a *shiur* four times! On occasion, he was so weak he would collapse on his bed from exhaustion. As soon as he felt a little better, though, he would sit up and learn. He would explain that, though he still felt very ill, his feeling slightly better was enough to spur him on to learn more.

✦ ✦ ✦

✦ At the funeral of Rav Mordechai Leib Zaks, his childhood friend Rav Elimelech Bar-Shaul, Rav of Rechovot, eulogized him. He described how they had learned together in Yeshivas Eitz Chaim under extremely difficult conditions — in dire poverty and with great suffering. His eulogy was followed by that of Rav Shmuel Aharon Yudelevitch, who said, "I, too, was in that same group in Eitz Chaim, but I must disagree with the Rav. It is true we studied Torah under impoverished conditions, but there was no suffering at all. Quite the contrary, we learned with great joy!"

The serious student understands that there are other advantages to suffering, in that it atones for one's sins. A wise person will thus not wait for Hashem to send suffering, but rather he will accept a lesser form of suffering on his own by toiling in Torah (which naturally weakens a person),[1] and by foregoing a life of luxury.

✦ Rav Shach wrote a letter of encouragement to a young American Rosh Yeshivah who was suffering from a painful terminal illness. He explained that were a person to realize how valuable a commodity suffering is, he would welcome the pain with open arms. Although that might be too difficult for most people, a person should nonetheless

1 See *Sanhedrin* 26b.

try to appreciate the suffering he has already endured, for through it he has amassed a great fortune in merits.

Suffering can also strengthen the bond between man and Hashem, when one views it as a means of communication from Hashem, prodding him to improve his behavior (*Igros* of the Chazon Ish).

Rav Isser Zalman Meltzer explained the way in which we can appreciate suffering with a parable. A father was walking with his son through a dark forest, when the son wandered off and became lost. It was impossible to see a thing, and the boy was very frightened. Suddenly, he felt a stinging slap across his face and his father angrily shouted, "Why did you wander off?" Painful though the slap was, the boy could not have been more comforted by his father's presence. Similarly, although Hashem may deem it necessary to punish us when we wander from the proper path, there is still comfort in the realization of Hashem's taking note of us.

Plan: ✦ *Accept suffering without complaint, recognizing that suffering can be an opportunity for spiritual growth and a means by which to accrue great reward.*

24 RECOGNIZING ONE'S PLACE

מכיר את מקומו

Every individual has his own strengths and weaknesses, and it is important that one recognize both. One who overestimates his capabilities, for example, will often fool himself regarding his understanding of Torah, and thus make mistakes in interpretation (*Derech Chaim*). For this reason, at Sinai the Jewish people were warned to remain in their designated places, and not to approach any closer than they had been instructed (see *Rashi* on *Shemos* 19:22). This command had symbolic, as well as physical, meaning. Recognizing one's place is thus a prerequisite for Torah (*Alei Shur*).

> ◆ Rav Yeruchem Levovitz, the Mashgiach of Mir, said that a person who does not recognize his faults cannot work to correct them. However, a person who does not appreciate his strengths lacks the tools with which to correct himself.

◆ ◆ ◆

✦ A student in the Ponovezh Yeshivah mastered the *Shulchan Aruch* in three and a half years. Upon his examination, he went to the Ponovezher Rav to receive his blessing. The Rav told his student, "You have learned over the past few years how to answer questions when you know the answer. But, you have not yet learned how to answer when you do not know the answer... I will not give you my blessings until you sit in the room at the side, and repeat to yourself one hundred times the words, 'I do not know.' Only then will I offer you my blessings."

Rav Shlomo Wolbe warns that one is only capable of recognizing his own strengths and weaknesses through the intensive study of *mussar*, and by staying focused on fulfilling one's mission (cited in *Mishel HaAvos*).

Another interpretation of "recognizing one's place" is understanding that one's true place is in *Olam HaBa*, since this world is only a temporary dwelling place. A person who understands that the only goal of everlasting value is in an afterlife, will spend the majority of his time in spiritual pursuit, such as Torah study (*Midrash Shmuel*).

✦ A wealthy businessman from England once visited the Chafetz Chaim in Radin. He was shocked to see the sparse furnishings in the great sage's home. He said to the Chafetz Chaim, "*Rebbi*, I imagined such a great personality would have a beautiful home. Where is your furniture?"

The Chafetz Chaim responded in kind. "And where is your furniture?"

The businessman replied, "My beautiful furniture is at home. Here I have nothing to show, for I am only a guest passing through."

"Ah!" smiled the sage, "I, too, am only a guest passing through!"

Rav Yosef Leib Bloch, the Telzer Rav, related this parable: A group of people were emigrating from Russia to America. Before they could obtain entrance visas to America, however, they would be required to stay in France for a few weeks. Most of the emigrants began studying English to prepare for the move. One person, however, decided that he wanted to enjoy his time in France, and instead learned French. When they reached France, the proud man was the only one who could communicate with others, as he alone understood French. But when they finally reached America a few weeks later, the poor fellow realized his mistake. Whereas everyone else was able to get settled and find work, he lacked the necessary language skills. The lesson is clear: A person must remain focused on "learning the language of *Olam HaBa*," and not be distracted by the glitter of the temporal world.

Another explanation of the term "recognizing one's place," is that one should have a designated place in the *beis midrash* where he studies regularly, a place he can recognize as his own. One who only visits the *beis midrash* occasionally does not have a seat he can call his own (*Midrash Shmuel*).

Plan: ✦ *Learn to appreciate one's strengths and weaknesses in order to develop potential.*

✦ *Remember not to be distracted by the attractions of this world, but remain focused on Olam HaBa.*

✦ *Designate a special place to learn in the beis midrash.*

25 HAPPINESS WITH ONE'S LOT

שמח בחלקו

O ne who loves money will never be satisfied with money" (*Koheles* 5:9). The desire for money is a powerful force that can control a person and pull him away from Torah study. A person who is satisfied with what he has will not be tempted by a desire for money (*Midrash Shmuel*).

✦ Rav Zusha Valtner was a student of Rav Eliyahu Dessler in Gateshead, England. One Friday, Reb Zusha mentioned to Rav Dessler that he was going shopping. When Rav Dessler asked if he could come along, Reb Zusha happily agreed. At a silver store, Reb Zusha excitedly viewed a beautiful tray for a very reasonable price. Just as he was about to purchase it, Rav Dessler indicated that he would like it for himself. He paid for it and put it in his bag. Sometime later, they saw a silver menorah that Reb Zusha wanted to purchase. Again, Rav Dessler claimed he wanted the menorah and bought it. This scene was repeated a third time with an exquisite *becher*. Reb Zusha began to feel resentful and regretted having his *rebbi* accompany him.

Shortly before Shabbos, Rav Dessler appeared at the Valtner's door with a package containing the tray, the menorah, and the cup. "These are a gift for you. I observed how excited you became when you first spotted these pieces. I wanted you to learn discipline, not to rush after material possessions. Silver is not something to get excited about."

Those who study Torah should be appreciative of their lot in life; it is far more valuable than the greatest material wealth (*Midrash Shmuel*). Even if one is not very successful in his learning, the mere fact that he has the merit to study Torah is in itself reason for satisfaction. No physical or material pleasure in the world can bring a person the joy and satisfaction that Torah study brings.

✦ A wealthy individual approached Rav Aharon Leib Steinman with a query. Most of his friends drove fancy expensive cars, and he was feeling pressure to conform to their style and buy a more expensive car. He asked the Rosh Yeshivah if he should be concerned that buying such a car would draw attention to himself and incur others' envy.

In response, Rav Steinman asked the man if he had yet mastered *Shas*. The man shook his head in amazement. "Of course not," he said.

"What about an entire *maseches*?" the Rosh Yeshivah asked. The answer again was in the negative.

"What about a chapter of Talmud?" Somewhat embarrassed, the man whispered, "No."

"Then I can't see any problem in buying the car," the Rosh Yeshivah responded incredulously. "I can't imagine why anyone would be jealous of you!"

One who realizes the great value of Torah study will not be bothered by any material deficiency. Material lack is always overshadowed by having the Torah and an accompanying relationship with Hashem. Rabbi Abraham Twerski draws an analogy to this. When a person suffering from a headache learns he has just won the lottery, the joy of winning makes him forget his headache. Similarly, a person's material deficiencies are completely eclipsed by the spritual riches he accrues by learning Torah.

Another interpretation of this quality refers to one's spiritual lot. Each person is endowed with the tools necessary for his own spiritual accomplishment. Some people are blessed with greater intelligence than others, some with better memories, and some with quicker comprehension. One should not be jealous of another's capacity for learning, since, in Heaven, success is measured by the degree one has actualized one's potential, irrespective of one's objective achievement or status. What another person accomplishes is not part of the picture. Furthermore, when one rejoices in his own accomplishments, he is driven to accomplish even more (*Cheshev HaEfod*).

> Rav Naftali Amsterdam once mentioned to Rav Yisrael Salanter, "*Rebbi*, if only I had your sterling character traits, the genius of the Sha'agas Aryeh, and the intense devotion of the Yesod V'Shoresh HaAvodah — how great I could be!"
>
> "No, Reb Naftali," Reb Yisrael replied. "With your character traits, your brain, and your heart — you can accomplish greatness."

Plan: ✦ *Be satisfied with one's material lot in life.*
   ✦ *Appreciate one's good fortune in being able to learn Torah.*
   ✦ *Be satisfied with G-d-bestowed capabilities, using them to the full.*

26 MAKE A FENCE FOR ONE'S WORDS

העושה סייג לדבריו

A person must be guarded in his speech, especially when conveying words of Torah, as they could be easily misconstrued (*Machzor Vitri*).[1] A Torah scholar must be especially careful with his words, since they are often analyzed by others; the Torah scholar's words set the standard. One who weighs each word carefully before he speaks, and only says what he believes, will benefit others and will never regret his words (*Orchos Yosher*).

✦ During the days of the Julius and Ethel Rosenberg trial in America, many prominent rabbis pleaded for clemency on behalf of the couple suspected of selling nuclear secrets to the Soviet Union. One newspaper reported that the Chazon Ish had personally asked the President to pardon the couple. When questioned about this, the Chazon Ish denied any such conversation. Yet, he refused to publicly

---

1   Although this may overlap parts of no. 17, "Minimal Conversation," see *Cheshev HaEfod* for differences.

distance himself from the story. "If I deny any involvement in this matter," he explained, "the Communists will accuse me of being callous to the plight of fellow Jews. And if I publicly express my sympathy for their plight, others will accuse me of being sympathetic to the Communists. I'm better off not responding to the story at all."

Lengthy interpretations can be confusing, both for the teacher and the student, and should thus be avoided (*Derech Chaim*). The Talmud relates that the sons of Yehudah were precise in their learning, and their Torah was thus preserved (*Eiruvin* 53a).

◆ I once invited a well-known Rav to deliver a class for an hour. After forty-five minutes, however, he brought his words to a close. I urged the Rav to continue speaking for the remaining time. The Rav smiled and said, "That reminds me of the *shochet* who would use an unusually short knife to slaughter. When questioned as to why he used such a short knife, he explained that for the part of the knife that was missing, nobody could find any disqualification. Similarly, nobody can have any complaints on the part of a speech left unsaid."

The Mishnah advises that silence is a fence to protect wisdom (*Avos* 3:13). Only a fool feels the need to contribute something to every conversation. A wise man understands when something needs to be said and when something need not be said (Chazon Ish in *Pe'er Hador*).

Rav Refoel of Hamburg said, "Not everything one thinks should be spoken; not everything one speaks should be written; and not everything one writes should be published" (this is also said over in the name of Rav Yisrael Salanter).

The "protective fences" may also refer to fences erected to

prevent transgression of Torah law. Chazal enacted several ordinances, such as *muktzah*, in order to avoid transgressing the laws of Shabbos. The Torah personality must recognize his own weaknesses and then create personal fences to avoid being vulnerable to temptation (*Midrash Shmuel*). A person who has a true fear of sin will do everything he possibly can to steer clear of sin.

Plan: ✦ *Use words — even words of Torah — sparingly, concisely, and clearly, in order that they not be misconstrued.*

✦ *Take protective measures to avoid transgressing the Torah's prohibitions.*

27 NOT TAKING CREDIT FOR ONESELF

אינו מחזיק טובה לעצמו

One who understands the importance and necessity of Torah in his life will invest all his efforts to plumb its depths. Such a person does not seek compliments and honor for his work. He knows that he is merely doing what is required of him. The Mishnah teaches, "If you have learned much Torah, do not take credit for it, for that is why you were created" (*Avos* 2:8; see *Rashi* ad loc.). Just as one does not take pride in eating or sleeping well — as these are necessary for a healthy living — one must not take pride in Torah study, which is essential for a healthy soul (Chafetz Chaim, cited in *Tenuas HaMussar*).

✦ Rav Shach was once in the hospital for an operation. He overheard some family members planning to tell the hospital staff who their important patient was and ask that he be treated accordingly. Rav Shach protested strongly: "I am no different than any other old man. The doctors are paid to treat all their patients equally. Were they to treat me differently from anyone else, it would be at the expense of the other patients, and that would be stealing!"

✦ ✦ ✦

✦ The Chafetz Chaim's son, Reb Leib, asked his father if he thought people could ever appreciate the years of exertion and toil he had put into writing every page of the *Mishnah Berurah*. The Chafetz Chaim responded, "Why should it bother me if people don't appreciate my work properly? Did I work so hard just to earn people's praise? Hashem could testify that my intentions were only for His glory — and He surely knows the effort that went into the *Mishnah Berurah*."

Even when a person has achieved success in Torah knowledge, he must realize that without the assistance of Hashem, he could not accomplish anything (*Lechem Shamayim*).

✦ Rav Shlomo Wolbe, author of *Alei Shur* — a work that Rav Yechezkel Levenstein considered obligatory reading for every yeshivah student — once remarked, "It often happens that an author is unable to express his greatness through his writing, and the book does not do justice to its author. In *Alei Shur*, however, the opposite is true. There was so much assistance in its writing from Above, that the resulting book is actually greater than its author...."

A person should also realize that, despite all the effort and toil he puts into Torah study, ultimately, his understanding is but a gift from Hashem (*Ruach Chaim*). Regarding Torah study, the Talmud says that if a person insists that he put in effort but did not find the right interpretation of what he learned, one should not believe him. If, however, he claims that he put forth effort and did find the right interpretation, he should be believed (*Megillah* 6b). The Vilna Gaon explains that the intention of the Gemara is that even after one puts in the effort, the understanding one attains still remains a "find" or a gift.

✦ In his earlier years in the Slutzk Yeshivah, though diligent in his studies, Rav Pesach Pruskin was not known as a brilliant scholar. Once, he excitedly shared an original insight on a section of *Bava Kama* with some of the other scholars. They chided him, saying that the insight was not well thought-out. Reb Pesach was heartbroken. He ran to another room and cried until he fell asleep. He dreamed that he should not give up, and that if he would begin to study *Bava Kama* again, he would enjoy great success. Upon waking, Rav Pesach felt an infusion of strength. He immediately tackled the text with renewed vigor. Lo and behold, he understood the Gemara with a depth and clarity he had not previously experienced. His insights earned the respect of the Torah world.

Plan: ✦ *Remember that success in Torah is only a gift from Hashem.*
✦ *Remember that the purpose of toil is not to impress others, but rather to fulfill Hashem's will.*

28 BE BELOVED

אהוב

person with sterling character traits earns both Hashem's love and the love of his fellow beings (*Lechem Shamayim*). Being loved in both ways is important for the goal of acquiring Torah. Hashem assists those He loves and helps them better understand His Torah (*Derech Chaim*); similarly, one's contemporaries share their knowledge with one whom they love (*Midrash Shmuel; Cheshev HaEfod*).

The Talmud says of the passage, "You should love Hashem your G-d " (*Devarim* 6:5) that one should cause Hashem's name to be beloved through his actions (*Yoma* 86a). It is inspiring to note how careful our *gedolim* have always been in their consideration and sensitivity towards others. Despite their gruelling schedules and constant involvement in Torah study and other important matters, they would make the time and effort to give of themselves to others. By their enhancing Hashem's glory in the eyes of others, Hashem, in kind, enhances their own greatness in Torah.

✦ At the funeral of Rav Yaakov Kaminetzky, many people were surprised to see a nun in attendance. When questioned regarding her connection with the Rosh Yeshivah, she explained that Reb Yaakov would take a daily walk past her residence. Although the other Jewish neighbors rarely acknowledged her, the elderly Rosh Yeshivah never failed to nod at the nun and wish her a good morning. She was so impressed with the Rosh Yeshivah's courtesy, that when she heard of his passing, she wanted to pay her respects.

◆ ◆ ◆

✦ An African-American painter noticed a picture of the Bobover Rebbe, Rav Shlomo Halberstam, hanging on the wall of a customer. "That's my rabbi, too!" he proudly said, pulling out a similar picture from his wallet. The painter explained that he had done some work in the Rebbe's house. Every morning when he arrived, the Rebbe would ask him if he had eaten breakfast yet. If he had not yet eaten, some food and drink would be brought out before he started working.

◆ ◆ ◆

✦ When Rav Shlomo Wolbe travelled by bus, he would generally sit at the front of the bus, deep in thought and seemingly oblivious to the noise about him. One day, a young man boarded the bus and began playing his violin. (The fellow was clearly not quite normal.) The other passengers either ignored the fellow or snickered, making disparaging remarks about the young man's music. Before alighting, Rav Wolbe walked over to the man and gently said, "Thank you for making the ride more enjoyable."

Another interpretation of being "beloved" is studying the Torah purely for the sake of the mitzvah. This is called learning Torah *lishmah*. The Talmud teaches that one who studies Torah *lishmah* is called "beloved" (*Avos* 6:1). Learning Torah *lishmah* creates a special bond between a person and Hashem. This bond allows the person to acquire *da'as Torah*, the unique Torah outlook on life (*Cheshev HaEfod*).

✦A man came to ask Rav Elchanan Wasserman, Rosh Yeshivah of Baranovitch, for his advice on a complicated business-related issue. After carefully listening to the man's query, Reb Elchanan took out a Gemara and began to learn by himself. The bewildered man just sat quietly, not sure exactly what to do. After a little while, Reb Elchanan closed his Gemara and offered the man his advice. When asked why he hadn't said anything right away, Reb Elchanan explained, "When I am faced with a question I feel needs *da'as Torah*, I first try to prepare myself by learning *Torah lishmah*. Only then do I feel confident enough to offer advice."

Plan: ✦ *Behave in a way that will earn Hashem's love.*
   ✦ *Create a kiddush Hashem in dealings with other people.*
   ✦ *Learn Torah with pure motivations.*

29 LOVE HASHEM

אוהב את המקום

The Torah says, "You should love Hashem your G-d " (*Devarim* 6:5). These words instruct every Jew to love Hashem. The Rambam (*Sefer HaMitzvos* 3) and the *Sefer HaChinuch* (418) explain that this love is developed when we delve into the Torah. Torah study is also an expression of our love for Hashem. Conversely, the more we love Hashem, the more that love is reciprocated — and Hashem expresses His love by opening our minds so that we understand the Torah and are able to unlock its secrets (*Midrash Shmuel*).

Rav Abba Grossbard, the Mashgiach of Ponovezh Yeshivah, noted that the Rambam, in his commentary on the Mishnah, often begins with "Hashem Yisbarach says...." The Rambam is trying to convey the inextricable identification of Hashem with the Torah. Hashem wants us to feel a strong connection to the Torah, and through the Torah we will feel close to Hashem, too (cited in *Mishel HaAvos*).

Elsewhere, the Rambam says that one can develop love for Hashem by studying the beauty and intricacies of nature (*Yesodei HaTorah* 2:2). The more we study the world around us, the greater our amazement — and ultimately our appreciation — for the Creator.

Rav Mordechai Gifter often related a parable from Rav Mordechai Pogremanski, in order to explain the seeming inconsistency in the Rambam concerning the method by which to acquire love of G-d. Two friends visited the Louvre in Paris. While Yosef was admiring the beautiful works of da Vinci, Rembrandt, and other great artists, his friend Chaim seemed unimpressed. "This picture looks like sour milk, and so does that one!" he exclaimed.

"Wait a second," Yosef said to his friend. "Let me see your glasses." Chaim removed his glasses and showed them to Yosef. "Aha! Just as I thought. Your glasses are smeared with sour milk. No wonder everything looks like sour milk!"

The study of nature can, indeed, lead to love of Hashem — but only if viewed through a lens generated by Torah study (heard from Rav Gifter).

A person must strive to place his love for Hashem above all else, and not allow his love for physical and material pleasures to interfere with his love for Hashem (*Sefer HaChinuch* 418).

✦ After the war, the Klausenberger Rebbe found himself in one of the D.P. camps. Despite all the hardships and tragedies he had suffered during the war, the Rebbe remained a bulwark of strength and inspiration to all those around him. Even the camp administration recognized the Rebbe's greatness, and they would often go out of their way to help him. The cook was once making breakfast and he remarked to the Rebbe, "Rabbi, these potatoes are delicious! I love them cooked with pepper like this. How about you?"

The Rebbe immediately responded, "Love potatoes? Love pepper? I love Hashem, not potatoes and pepper!"

✦ ✦ ✦

✦ Rav Shimon Schwab, the Rav of the German-Jewish community in Washington Heights, recalled that when he was a young boy, his father asked the children at the Seder which of the four sons they wanted to emulate. The five young boys all answered they wanted to be like the wise son. Their father looked pleased. But then he looked at them seriously and said, "If any of my sons were to become the wicked son, I would tell him he has no place at my Seder table, because although I love you dearly, I love Hashem more than I love you." Then he resumed the Seder in his normal, gentle manner. Years later, the sons still felt the impact of that statement (*Selected Speeches*, p. 102).

Plan: ✦ *Develop love for Hashem by learning His Torah and by observing His world and all its beauty.*
✦ *Remember that love for Hashem must supersede all other love.*

30 LOVE
MANKIND

אוהב את הבריות

uman beings are Hashem's highest achievement. Therefore, loving people is an expression of love for Hashem (*Lechem Shamayim*).
The Ba'al Shem Tov said that loving our fellow is a vehicle for developing our love for
Hashem; the more we love Hashem's creatures, the more we
will love Him (*Ohr Yitzchak, parashas Toldos*). This love is also a
prerequisite for acquiring Torah, because the Torah was given to
the entire Jewish people, not merely to individuals. When a person loves a fellow Jew, he identifies himself as part of the Jewish
people. He thus deserves to receive the Torah (*Derech Chaim*).

◆ Rav Baruch Ber Leibovitz, the Kaminetzer Rosh
Yeshivah and a scholar of great renown, said, "When I
come before the Heavenly court and they ask me what I
have accomplished, what will I say? That I learned Torah?
Can I say that I learned Torah adequately? Have I achieved
proper fear of Heaven? But one thing I could say: I loved

my fellow Jews. Whenever I see a Jew in the street, I wish him all Hashem's blessings!"

No person is perfect, but everyone has certain qualities for which he can be appreciated, regardless of his flaws. Even when a person behaves in an evil manner, he should not be hated, although it may be necessary to hate the person's behavior. "One who loves Hashem, hates evil" (*Tehillim* 97:10) the *pasuk* tells us; however, this is an injunction to despise evil per se, but never the individual, who is created in the image of Hashem (*Lechem Shamayim, Tomer Devorah*, ch. 2). Hating the person merely arouses more hatred and negativity within oneself (*Ohr Yechezkel*).

⬥ Rav Yerucham Levovitz described how the countenance of Reb Simcha Zissel, the Alter of Kelm, would shine on Shabbos. One Shabbos, however, his students noticed that the Alter's face seemed dark. After Shabbos, they asked him why he had looked so distressed. The Alter sighed deeply and explained that Peretz Smolanskin, a *maskil* known for his vehement hatred of the religious community, had died. "Oy," he lamented, "it pains me so much to imagine the suffering of such a soul when it appears before its Maker!"

⬥ ⬥ ⬥

⬥ Rav Aryeh Levine, the tzaddik of Jerusalem, heard about a person who refused to close his store on Shabbos, despite the protests of the religious neighborhood. One Friday afternoon, Reb Aryeh entered the man's business and sat down at the side, without saying a word. The man asked Reb Aryeh a few times if he wanted something, but Reb Aryeh just smiled. Finally, the owner asked Reb Aryeh why he had come. Reb Aryeh answered, "I have heard that you keep your store open on Shabbos, and this really bothers me. I wanted to see for myself how difficult it must be for you to overcome the temptation to close your store for Shabbos." The man was so touched by Reb Aryeh's sensitivity that he promised to close his store on Shabbos.

Showing love and concern for a fellow Jew is also a prerequisite for bringing others closer to Torah. As the Mishnah teaches, "Love people and bring them close to Torah" (*Avos* 1:12). Furthermore, the reward for one who helps others study Torah is that he will acquire Torah as well (*Midrash Shmuel*).

✦ The Ponovezher Rav asked a wealthy benefactor what motivated his generosity to yeshivahs, since he was not personally observant. The man recalled how, as a youth, he was sent to the Chafetz Chaim's yeshivah in Radin. The boy had not been very interested in learning, and was not accepted into the yeshivah. The Chafetz Chaim, however, invited the frightened boy to sleep in his own house for the night. The young boy had a hard time falling asleep. During the night he heard the Chafetz Chaim enter the room and cover him with his own overcoat, to make sure he was warm enough. Although many years had passed since that incident, the man was still warmed by the Chafetz Chaim's concern, and he felt obliged to support yeshivahs.

Plan: ✦ *Find something positive in each person in order to love him.*
✦ *Help others, both with their spiritual and physical needs.*

31 LOVE RIGHTEOUSNESS

אוהב את הצדקות

Simply put, *tzedakah* refers to the assistance a person offers to those who are destitute. One who loves *tzedakah* does not merely help those who approach him; he actively pursues opportunities to help others in need. This was the characteristic of Avraham Avinu, who sat in the heat of the day shortly after his circumcision, seeking out needy wayfarers.

It is not clear exactly how this quality relates to acquiring Torah,[1] but some suggest, based on the Maharal (*Gevuros Hashem*, ch.5), that through *tzedakah* one acquires Divine levels of greatness, and is thus deserving of Divine wisdom (*Cheshev HaEfod*). Another interpretation is that even if one has achieved greatness in Torah study and scholarship, it is not a sufficient "acquisition" unless he also loves *tzedakah*.

◆ Rav Chaim Kreisworth, the Rav of Antwerp, was

---

1 Indeed, the Gra and *Midrash Shmuel* do not include "Loving Righteousness" among the forty-eight qualities.

renowned for his genius and great scholarship. Nonetheless, he spent an extraordinary amount of time raising funds for widows and for needy brides. An acquaintance who saw him running around for hours trying to collect money, was bothered by what he perceived as something beneath the Rav's dignity. "Couldn't you delegate the fundraising to others?" he asked. "The world would benefit more from your learning than from your fundraising activities!"

Rav Kreisworth smiled. "On the contrary! When I meet my Maker I am concerned He will tell me that other people could also have learned Torah, but not everyone is cut out for fundraising. This might be my purpose in this world!"

There is another meaning of *tzedakah* — the word could be derived from the word *tzedek*, meaning "justice." Loving righteousness means appreciating fairness, fighting the injustices of the world, and assisting the weak and oppressed. This quality was found in Moshe, who rescued the daughters of the former idolatrous priest, Yisro, from their antagonists, without ever having met them before (*Tiferes Yisrael*).

◆ The son of a wealthy man in Kovno was conscripted into the army. Through his connections, the man convinced the local authorities to instead take another young man, the son of a widow. The distraught woman burst into shul on Shabbos morning during the Torah reading, wailing about her plight. Some of the men tried to silence the woman, so that they could proceed with the Torah reading. Rav Yisrael Salanter, who was present at the time, was terribly upset at the men's callousness towards the woman. "You are so meticulous about performing other mitzvos, yet you allow this injustice to take place? Your prayers and

Torah reading at this time are meaningless!" Rav Yisrael castigated them. He left the shul and finished praying by himself.

✦ ✦ ✦

✦ A Rav once asked the Chazon Ish about a couple of teenagers who had been amusing themselves, and the young man gave the young woman a ring, pretending to marry her. The question at hand was whether the action would be considered a valid marriage, requiring a divorce before the woman would be allowed to marry. The Chazon Ish pondered the particulars of the question, and he then responded that no divorce was required. The Rav was surprised and expressed his reservation: since the issue of permitting a possibly married woman to marry is so serious, shouldn't a divorce be required out of doubt? The Chazon Ish responded, "And causing shame to a Jewish woman by requiring a divorce is not a serious issue to you?"

Plan: ✦ *Pursue opportunities to help others without infringing too much on Torah study.*
   ✦ *Champion the cause of the oppressed and respond meaningfully to other injustices of the world.*

32 LOVE
CHASTISEMENT
אוהב את התוכחות

Everyone errs occasionally, but only the person who is open to criticism will be able to to rectify his mistakes. The Torah personality actually welcomes criticism, as we learn in *Mishlei* (9:8) "Chastise the wise and he will love you" (*Rashi; Tiferes Yisrael*).

✦ The Vilna Gaon would occasionally summon Rav Yaakov Kranz, the Dubno Maggid, and instruct him to offer words of rebuke. "Everybody else is afraid to chastise me," he complained to the Maggid, "You are the only one who is willing to point out my flaws to me, and I truly appreciate your friendship."

✦ ✦ ✦

✦ A young scholar had criticized a ruling of Rav Moshe Feinstein. Later, he apologized for his seeming lack of respect in criticizing one of the foremost authorities of his generation. Reb Moshe responded to the challenge in a published responsa, where he wrote, "and regarding your concern that your words might have insulted me — quite to the contrary; it is reassuring to know that there are still people these days who are not afraid or embarrassed to offer words of reproof where they feel it is necessary" (*Igros Moshe, Even HaEzer*, vol.2, p. 322).

✦ ✦ ✦

✦When the Imrei Emes, Rav Avraham Mordechai Alter, was a young boy, he was once late for his morning *shiur*. His father, the Sefas Emes, sharply rebuked the boy for several minutes about the severity of not taking Torah study seriously. A friend who had studied with Avraham Mordechai through the previous night, asked him afterwards, "Why didn't you tell your father about your all-night session? I'm sure he would have understood."

"Why should I give up an opportunity to hear words of reproof from my father about the importance of Torah study?" the future Gerrer Rebbe responded.

The serious student of Torah concerns himself not only with his own behavior, but with the behavior of others, as well. Therefore, he offers words of chastisement when he feels they are needed (*Midrash Shmuel*).

It is interesting that the plural form of chastisement — *tochachos* — is used here, because two forms of criticism are necessary. A person must first appreciate receiving criticism of his own behavior before he can criticize others. This is necessary because it shows that the reproof is coming from one who is sincere, rather than one who simply has the desire to criticize (*Ruach Chaim*). Alternatively, one should include himself in his words of reproach to others, because they will then have a greater impact (*Beis Aharon*, cited in *Memeinos HaNetzach*).

✦ A group of students asked the Chafetz Chaim to give them words of *mussar*. The Chafetz Chaim sighed and said, "How could I criticize others when I am such a lowly sinner, lacking both Torah knowledge and fear of Hashem?" The few simple words of their *rebbi*'s self-criticism inspired the students more than any discourse.

Many of the *maggidim* of old would begin their *derashos* with the refrain, "I am not worthy of offering criticism to others. Instead, I will criticize myself, aloud; and if anyone else will also be inspired by my words, I will have accomplished more than I have set out to do!"

Words of reproof must be offered in a gentle manner so they can be accepted. Criticism given in a harsh or cynical manner usually accomplishes little. Thus, a nervous, impatient person who cannot chastise others gently is exempt from the mitzvah, just as one who has no arm is exempt from laying tefillin (Rav Chaim Volozhiner cited in *Keser Rosh*).

Plan: ✦ *Welcome reproof, viewing it as an aid to personal improvement.*
  ✦ *Offer gentle constructive criticism to others.*

33 LOVE
HONESTY

אוהב את המישרים

The Torah is a doctrine of truth. The acquisition of Torah, then, requires an appreciation for honesty, both in one's interactions with others and within oneself (*Lechem Shamayim; Cheshev HaEfod*). A person who is honest in his relationship with others (not resorting to flattery, for example), and who is honest in his business dealings, will approach Torah study with that same integrity. Such a person merits a true understanding of Torah (*Midrash Shmuel*).

◆ Rav Baruch Ber Leibovitz studied in Volozhin under Rav Chaim Soloveichik. Once, he was engaged in an halachic debate with Rav Avraham Kagan, the Chafetz Chaim's son. They asked Reb Chaim for his opinion. Reb Chaim concurred with Reb Avraham. Later, Reb Chaim remarked to Reb Baruch Ber, "Do you really think you could win Reb Avraham in a Torah discussion? Coming from a home that excels in integrity and righteousness, he receives special Divine assistance with his Torah study!"

The Torah student's concern for honesty drives him to concern himself even with other people's dealings.[1] Thus, we find (*Bereishis* 29:7, see *Seforno*) Yaakov, who personified Torah study,[2] chastising the shepherds in Padan Aram for sitting idly during daylight hours, thereby stealing time from their employers (*Alei Be'er*).

✦ The Brisker Rav, Rav Velvel Soloveichik, would not accept financial assistance from any person whose money was tainted by sin — both those sins committed between man and Hashem and those committed between man and man. He said that no success could come from Torah study supported by such funds.

Torah study itself calls for an unrelenting quest for truth. When studying Torah, one should search for the simple and clear interpretation, and avoid illogical or forced explanations, tempting though they may be (*Tiferes Yisrael*).

✦ Rav Shlomo Heiman, Rosh Yeshivah in Baranovich and later at Torah Vodaath, worked at training his students to think *glatt*, in a straight and clear manner. When his students would suggest an answer to an *Acharon*'s question, he would often tell them, "For this question it is not necessary to offer an answer; you must try to understand why the question cannot even begin!"

✦ ✦ ✦

✦ Rav Tzvi Pesach Frank, the Rav of Yerushalayim, would encourage his students to have a set *seder* to

---

1 See *Mishlei* (29:27): "The righteous are repulsed by the man of deceit."
2 See *Bereishis* (25:27): "And Yaakov was a perfect man, who dwelled in tents," and *Rashi* ad loc.

learn *Ketzos HaChoshen* and *Nesivos HaMishpat*, because he felt these *sefarim* could help straighten the minds of his students. That way, they could gain a true understanding of Torah. The Chazon Ish encouraged students to learn the Maharsha's commentary for the same reason.

✦ ✦ ✦

✦ There was a shochet in Brisk named Reb Noach Prager, who would record Rav Chaim Soloveichik's lectures for him. Once, Rav Chaim paced back and forth for two hours, thinking and dictating his lecture to Reb Noach. The *shochet*'s hands were aching as he continued writing without stop. Rav Chaim paused, lost in thought for fifteen minutes. Suddenly, he turned to Reb Noach and said, "The whole idea is not *emes*!" and he took the papers and tore them up. Reb Noach protested, "*Rebbi*! Even if it might not be *emes* to your mind, most people wouldn't even be bothered by your problem. It's a shame on all my hard work!"

"No," Rav Chaim disagreed, "something that is not *emes* must not remain anywhere in the world."

Plan: ✦ *Be honest in all dealings, both with others and with Hashem.*
✦ *Think simply and logically, not resorting to illogical or contrived interpretations in learning.*

34 FLEE FROM HONOR

מתרחק מן הכבוד

Torah study is primarily a means of expressing one's love for Hashem and connecting with Him (*Midrash Shmuel*). One who studies Torah for personal reward — such as in order to gain stature or honor — does not accomplish either of these ends. Furthermore, one who studies for personal gain will not be able to focus completely on his studies; he will always be gauging what he stands to gain from his efforts (*Lechem Shamayim*).

✦ A student once came to the Steipler Gaon for his *berachah*, because he felt he was not succeeding in his studies. Before he even opened his mouth, however, the Steipler said, "Do you know why students get depressed about their learning? There is only one reason — because they are concerned about honor. They are bothered that the Rosh Yeshivah isn't impressed with them, that their friends understand the material better and ask better questions, and so forth. Their jealousy causes them to be depressed. If a student would learn with the right goal in mind — that when he appears before his Creator after 120 years, he shouldn't be embarrassed by his ignorance — he wouldn't be bothered by issues of honor, and there would be no reason for depression."

The Talmud tells us that one who pursues honor, honor will elude him; whereas one who flees from honor, honor will pursue him (*Eiruvin* 13b). Elsewhere we are taught that Torah represents the only true honor (*Avos* 6:3). Thus, only one who flees from honor will be able to acquire the honor of Torah (*Derech Chaim*).

✦ Rav Simcha Wasserman was a giant in Torah scholarship, yet he was an extremely humble man. In his later years, he lived in the Mattersdorf section of Jerusalem, where he davened at Yeshivas Torah Ohr. Although he was urged to sit in the front of the *beis midrash*, next to the Roshei Yeshivah, he refused and sat in the middle of the *beis midrash*, next to the young students.

One Sukkos, Reb Simcha attended a *simchas beis hasho'eivah*, where the Mashgiach, Rav Shlomo Wolbe, was speaking. As was his custom, he took a seat at the rear of the sukkah, among the students. Rav Wolbe spotted Reb Simcha and invited him to sit "on the *mizrach*," the so-called head table up front. Reb Simcha was clearly uncomfortable with the attention and waved his hand in refusal. "Nu, HaRav Wasserman, where you sit is the head table," Rav Wolbe told him. "If you don't come here, I must come to you!" When Reb Simcha saw Rav Wolbe actually moving towards him, he quickly stood up and moved to the head table.

Although there is an obligation to honor a Torah scholar, a scholar should be careful not to use his knowledge as a means for demanding honor (*Midrash Shmuel; Tiferes Yisrael*).

✦ Rav Yaakov Kaminetzky was revered as one of greatest Torah sages of recent times. When he attended Torah gatherings, Reb Yaakov always waited in the hallway before entering the room. Since he knew that those in the room would rise in his honor when he entered, he waited until he saw that everyone was standing anyway. Only then would he walk in, so that people didn't have to stand specifically for him.

✦ ✦ ✦

✦ When Rav Elya Meir Bloch founded the Telshe Yeshivah in Cleveland in 1941, very few of the American-bred boys understood what it meant to show proper respect to a Torah scholar. And so, the boys were instructed to stand up whenever the Roshei Yeshivah would pass them. Once, Reb Elya Meir passed a student who was sitting and studying. The student lifted his torso slightly from the chair, without even looking up. Suddenly, the young man felt a little kick in the seat of his pants. To his shock and chagrin, he saw the Rosh Yeshivah standing before him. "I realize this probably makes me look foolish in your eyes," Reb Elya Meir said, "but please don't think that I need you to stand up for me. Yet, what can I do? The Torah says that a student must show his *rebbi* proper respect, and it is my job to train you how to show that respect. Standing like that does not show respect!"

Plan: ✦ *Avoid honor, even as a response to accomplishment in Torah study.*
✦ *Focus on learning for the purpose of pleasing Hashem and not for personal gain.*

35 NOT BEING ARROGANT ABOUT ONE'S LEARNING

לא מגיס לבו בתלמודו

This character trait is a corollary of fleeing from honor. Not only must a person flee from seeking honor from others; he must also realize that his own Torah knowledge is far from complete. Regardless of what he has learned, it is but a drop in the ocean compared with what there is yet to learn (*Midrash Shmuel; Lechem Shamayim*). For this reason, Moshe Rabbeinu was able to be the most humble man on earth, despite receiving the Torah directly from Hashem in an experience of unparalleled revelation. Although his Torah knowledge was greater than anyone else's, so was his knowledge of how much more there was yet to know (*Zera Kodesh, Mo'adim*).

◆ A scholar once posed a few halachic queries in the laws of *kilayim*, prohibited hybridism, to Rav Isser Zalman

Meltzer. The Rosh Yeshivah said he did not feel qualified to answer the questions until he had done sufficient research. A short while later, Reb Isser Zalman wrote a lengthy response to the questions. In this response, he displayed tremendous depth and total command of the subject. The scholar was amazed by Reb Isser Zalman's earlier humility. He asked him why he had acted as though he was not proficient in this area, when that was clearly not the case. Reb Isser Zalman shrugged his shoulders and said, "Do you really think that is considered knowing the material well? There is still so much more I must learn in order to truly master the subject."

The Torah scholar also understands that whatever knowledge he acquires is a gift from Hashem, to be used for the right purpose: to bring glory to Hashem's Name. To be arrogant about one's Torah knowledge is as foolish as a bank teller bragging about the large sums of money in his hands — the money is not his own, but has merely been entrusted to him to give to the customers of the bank (*Chafetz Chaim*).

In a responsa, Chasam Sofer suggests that one who publishes Torah thoughts for the sake of self-aggrandizement actually transgresses the prohibition of committing the Oral Torah to writing (*Gittin* 60b). The only reason the Rabbis permitted writing the Torah is because they were concerned lest it be forgotten. They felt that it was an *eis la'asos laHashem*, a time to act for Hashem (*Tehillim* 119:126). However, if one's intentions are for personal gain, then the individual has no permission to write Torah, and, by doing so, transgresses this prohibition.

◆ In his youth, Rav Mendel of Vitebsk learned in the *beis midrash* of the Mezeritcher Maggid. One day, the Maggid witnessed the young man strutting about with his yarmulke cocked to one side of his head, pleased that he had covered six pages of Talmud, in depth, in one session. The Maggid wryly remarked, "Reb Mendel, if it takes six pages to push your yarmulke to the side, how many pages would it take to knock it off completely?" The young man was ashamed, and asked the Maggid how he should be learning. The Maggid then invited Reb Mendel to accompany him to the Ba'al Shem Tov, who would instruct him how to learn Torah with humility and purity.

Included in this characteristic is approaching Torah study with the proper reverence. An arrogant person thinks nothing of offering his own insights, even before he is certain of their veracity; the humble man, however, approaches Torah with trepidation and caution before suggesting an interpretation (*Tiferes Yisrael*). In fact, the Ramban begins his commentary on the Torah with the following words:

> I begin to write these insights on the Torah with feelings of awe, reverence, and fear. I pray and confess with a humble heart and a broken spirit, and ask for forgiveness and atonement.... My soul knows clearly that the difference between my limited and shallow understanding and the depths and hidden secrets of the Torah is greater than the difference between the egg of an ant and the great expanse of the heavenly planets....

Plan: ✦ *Remember that all Torah knowledge is a gift from Hashem; one has no right to be boastful.*
✦ *Realize that, regardless of accomplishments, there is always so much more to know.*

36 NOT

DELIGHTING IN
RENDERING
DECISIONS

אינו שמח בהוראה

The Mishnah warns that a man who is eager to render halachic decisions is foolish, wicked, and arrogant (*Avos* 4:7). He is foolish because he doesn't realize how easy it is to err in halachah. He is also wicked, because if his decision is erroneous, others may sin as a consequence. Furthermore, he voluntarily earns himself enemies by presumptuously issuing decisions (*Tiferes Yisrael*).

One who does not approach halachic decision making with caution, fear, and humility, shows careless disregard for the property of others: there is always the possibility that he will take money from its rightful owner and award it illegally to another person (*Midrash Shmuel*).

Being too self-confident of one's authority and judicial power is the height of arrogance. Such a person does not understand the importance of formulating a correct opinion — he is more interested in impressing people with his ability to adjudicate quickly (Rabbeinu Yonah; *Cheshev HaEfod*).

◆ Rav Isser Zalman Meltzer was offered the rabbinic post in Slutzk. He went to the Chafetz Chaim to discuss whether or not he should accept the position. He explained that he was nervous about assuming such a great responsibility. The Chafetz Chaim replied, "Who then should be offered the post? Someone who is not concerned about the responsibility? A Rav who fears Hashem should always be nervous about rendering halachic decisions!"

A person invested in Torah is always concerned about being sufficiently well-versed to make a ruling. He always worries that he might make a mistake (*Tiferes Yisrael*).

◆ Rav Moshe Feinstein was once asked a question, to which he responded with the opinion of the Shach, giving the specific chapter of the *Shulchan Aruch* and the citation number. A young scholar present interjected that he believed it was a different number, as he had just studied that commentary a little earlier. Reb Moshe was adamant, however. He would not continue until a *Shulchan Aruch* was brought, and he was able to check the page to make sure he was correct. He explained, "I am always careful to remember every citation number of the Shach. If, in my old age, I am beginning to forget the citation numbers, I do not feel qualified to render decisions."

◆ ◆ ◆

✦ Rav Isser Zalman Meltzer's son, Reb Refael Tzvi
Yehuda, described how his father would be literally
sick both the month before and the month after he offici-
ated at a *get*. On the day of the *get* itself, he could not eat at
all. Besides taking the pain of a broken marriage to heart,
he was nervous that the *get* be executed properly. The seri-
ousness of permitting a married woman to remarry
weighed heavily on his conscience.

One should certainly not be eager to render halachic decisions if there are greater experts available. One should only agree
to decide the halachah if it is absolutely necessary (*Lechem
Shamayim*).

✦ Rav Tzvi Pesach Frank, the Rav of Jerusalem, would always avail himself to answer halachic queries. However, when he felt the issue could be decided just as well by
other *rabbanim*, he discouraged people from turning to
him. "I don't need a mitzvah that could be performed by
others," he used to say.

✦ ✦ ✦

✦ Rav Naftali Amsterdam was reluctant to decide queries, even when he held a post in the rabbinate. He always discussed each question brought to him with his colleagues, especially with Rav Yitzchak Blauser. He explained that all a person's efforts at character development
are for naught if a person causes another to sin, even once,
by issuing an improper ruling.

Plan: ✦ *Be cautious before offering any opinion in
halachah.*
✦ *When it is necessary to offer a halachic opinion, do
not rush into any decision.*

37 SHARING THE BURDEN OF FRIENDS
נושא בעול עם חברו

The Torah student must develop a sensitivity to-wards others so that he begins to feel the pain of others as his own (*Midrash Shmuel*). This em-pathy is at the root of all the mitzvos between man and his fellow Jew. A person must feel an-other's need in order to be motivated to help. It is also an impor-tant part of emulating Hashem's ways, as the Torah relates, at Mount Sinai, "they saw the G-d of Israel, and under His feet was a brick of sapphire..." (*Shemos* 24:10). Rashi cites the Midrash to explain that this brick was from the Egyptian enslavement, and that Hashem kept it before Him at all times, as it were, in order to feel the pain of the Jewish people (*Alei Shur*, vol.1, p. 253).

✦ The Ponovezher Rav, Rav Yosef Kahaneman, was once traveling near Radin and decided to visit the famed Chafetz Chaim to receive his blessing. While waiting for the sage, Rav Kahaneman heard a loud groan coming from the Chafetz Chaim's room. Alarmed, he asked one of the family members if something was wrong. He was told that a man had just informed the Chafetz Chaim about his wife's serious medical condition. The Chafetz Chaim was so grieved for the couple's suffering that he couldn't control his cries. That was the noise Rav Kahaneman had heard. The Ponovezher Rav was so impressed with the Chafetz Chaim's empathy for another Jew that he decided to stay and learn under the great sage.

✦ ✦ ✦

Rav Avraham Grodzenski, the Mashgiach of Slabodka, was once seen in his summer lodging in an especially joyous mood. He told those around him that his friend was getting married that evening. Although he could not attend the *simchah*, Rav Grodzenski nonetheless wanted to join in the *simchah* from a distance. (A similar story is told about Rabbi Akiva Eiger.)

Sharing the burden of others includes sharing their burden of Torah — helping others resolve their questions and work through problems in Torah learning. The Talmud relates in several places how one *amora* would come to the defense of another, even if he personally disagreed with the other's opinion[1] (*Ruach Chaim*).

Whenever a student would discuss a Torah topic with Rav Nachum Partzovitz, the Mirrer Rosh Yeshivah, Reb Nachum would help the student clarify his position in such a way that the student walked away feeling as though he himself had crafted a beautiful piece of Torah. Even if the student merely asked a question, Reb Nachum would interject, "Ah, you mean to ask this? That's a wonderful

1 See *Bava Metzia* 22a and *Sukkah* 19a.

question — why didn't I think of that? But according to what you're saying, it could be answered like this; and with that idea we can answer the question of the Ketzos on the Rashba. You probably meant to prove that from the inference in Rashi...amazing...."

Bearing another's yoke can also mean accepting other people's character flaws and idiosyncrasies, even when they are trying and difficult to bear (*Midrash Shmuel*).

✦ Rav Yosef Ber Soloveichik author of the *Beis HaLevi*, was once asked a very simple halachic question by an elderly woman. Reb Yoshe Ber listened patiently and attentively as the woman elaborated on the question, giving a lengthy description that included totally unrelated details. When she had finished speaking, Reb Yoshe Ber took a volume from his shelf, perused it for a few minutes, and then responded to the woman's query. After the woman departed, the students, who had had a hard time keeping straight faces, asked their *rebbi* why he had wasted so much time listening to the drawn-out story when he could have answered the question immediately. Reb Yoshe Ber responded, "If I would not have shown this woman that I took her question seriously, perhaps when she would have a more complicated question, she would be ashamed to ask me."

Plan: ✦ *Develop the sensitivity to imagine and feel a friend's pain.*
   ✦ *Help share a friend's burden in Torah, and help him better understand his learning.*
   ✦ *Be patient and accepting of others' character flaws.*

38 JUDGING FAVORABLY

מכריעו לכף זכות

Giving others the benefit of the doubt is essential to maintaining any relationship. One who is suspicious of others will never be able to benefit from the wisdom of teachers or friends; he will always harbor doubts regarding whether his friends or teachers are sincere or whether they are motivated by self-interest (Rav Meir Lehmann, commentary to *Avos* 1:6).

✦ On a trip to Eretz Yisrael, a yeshivah student noticed a distinguished-looking person sitting near him on the plane. The *bachur* was disappointed to see that, although the man gave the appearance of being a *ben Torah*, he did not open a *sefer* the entire trip. When several people stood up to form a minyan, the man did not show any interest in participating — or in davening, either. In fact, he did not even *bench* after eating his meal. The *bachur* was upset; he felt the man must be a fraud. After the plane had landed and was nearly empty, the *bachur* noticed several people accompanying the man to the cargo section, where a coffin was lowered from the plane. Only then did he realize that the man had accompanied a deceased family member for burial. The man was an *onan*, and was thus precluded from studying Torah or davening.

One must also give the benefit of the doubt in matters of Torah study, in order to avoid shaming one who has erred in his reasoning or conclusions (*Lechem Shamayim*). Although truth may not be sacrificed, one must be careful not to rejoice or take pride in pointing out someone else's mistakes. Furthermore, even when someone's actions or opinions are incorrect, the person himself, whenever possible, should still be given the benefit of the doubt (Rav Yosef Chaim Sonnenfeld, cited in *Mishel HaAvos*).

⟡ A grandson of Rabbi Akiva Eiger sent him a letter with his original insights. In his response, Rabbi Akiva Eiger writes, "regarding that which you wrote.... I cannot understand these words, perhaps due to my limited capabilities. Believe me, I worked on understanding them for more than half an hour, but to no avail. I am troubled that perhaps my many activities and distractions have dulled my mind, Heaven forbid...." After trying unsuccessfully to justify his grandson's insight, Rabbi Akiva Eiger chose to fault himself, to attribute his lack of comprehension to his own shortcomings, rather than cause his grandson embarrassment.

✦ ✦ ✦

⟡ Rav Chaim Kreisworth, the Rav of Antwerp, once visited the Chazon Ish and told him an original insight that explained a contradiction in the Rambam. The Chazon Ish listened but did not comment. A while later, as the Chazon Ish escorted his guest to the door, he said to Rav Kreisworth, "By the way, your answer to the Rambam is incorrect." He then pointed out the error. Rav Kreisworth later commented that although the Chazon Ish could have corrected him immediately, he wanted to give the young scholar the benefit of the doubt, and allow him the time to recognize the error on his own. Only when he saw that Rav Kreisworth did not correct himself, did the Chazon Ish feel obligated to correct him.

Judging others favorably also means helping them take a flaw or negative action and transform it into something positive (*Derech Chaim*). Negative traits, such as anger, can be channeled positively and used constructively with the right guidance.

During the Alter from Slabodka's last days, his students would take turns caring for him and feeding him. One day, a student accidentally fed him a spoonful of alcohol instead of water. The Alter almost choked; he was unable to breathe, and only with difficulty was the doctor able to revive him. The student was understandably mortified. The Alter called the student to his bedside the next morning and said to him, "You gave me such pleasure yesterday! At first I was so frightened, but when I was able to breathe again, and I realized there was nothing to worry about, I experienced such joy! I must thank you for that!"

Plan: ✦ *Give others the benefit of the doubt, viewing their intentions favorably even when they are clearly wrong.*
✦ *Do not cause people unnecessary shame.*

39 GUIDE OTHERS TOWARDS TRUTH

מעמידו על האמת

The goal in studying Torah is to achieve ultimate truth. Truth, however, must not be kept to oneself; it must be shared with others. To allow others to remain uninformed or ignorant, when one has seen the truth himself, suggests that one's Torah study is self-serving, rather than being for the sake of clarifying truth (*Midrash Shmuel*).

◆ Towards the end of his life, Rav Avraham Pam, Rosh Yeshivah of Torah Vodaath, held a minyan in his home on Shabbos. One week, at *minchah*, the *chazan* erred in the repetition of the *Amidah*. Rav Pam told him to repeat the *berachah*. Later, Rav Pam pondered the matter and decided that it had not been necessary to repeat the *berachah*. After *ma'ariv*, Rav Pam announced that he had erred, and he stated the actual halachah. He noticed that his student, Rabbi Baruch Rabinowitz, had been at *minchah* but not at *ma'ariv*, so he called him and repeated

145

his correction. Then he told Rabbi Rabinowitz, "I want to be certain that no error in halachah comes from my home. Do you recall who else was there?" Rabbi Rabinowitz remembered one other neighbor who had been present at *minchah*, and offered to call him. The following Shabbos, as soon as that neighbor entered, Rav Pam asked him if he had received the message about his error.

+ + +

Reb Simcha Zissel of Kelm once passed a house from which he could hear someone singing *zemiros*. He noticed that the mystery singer missed out a few bars in his rendition of the song. Reb Simcha Zissel knocked on the door of the house. He informed the occupant that he felt it was his responsibility to correct him, as the mistaken rendition of the song was an aberration from truth.

One should try to guide and correct the mistakes of others tactfully, with the goal of maintaining both truth and peace (*Rashi*). If it is impossible to correct the other person gently, one has no choice but to speak sharply, in order to ensure that the mistake is rectified. One must never permit any misinterpretation of Torah to remain without comment (*Lechem Shamayim*).

Reb Yisrael Zev Gustman, Rosh Yeshivah of Yeshivas Netzach Yisrael, was renowned for his expertise in Torah. He once entertained a broken-spirited friend by reciting every *Tosafos* in *maseches Kiddushin* by heart, with various commentaries. On one occasion, an American student asked Rav Gustman a question on a *gemara* in *Kiddushin*. The Rosh Yeshivah replied, "I don't recall the *gemara* exactly. Please bring me a *sefer*; we'll learn through it together, and then we'll address your question." After studying the *gemara*, *Rashi* and *Tosafos* together, Rav

Gustman asked the student to repeat his question. The student realized then that his question had been based on a mistaken understanding of the *gemara*, and that the Rosh Yeshivah had feigned ignorance in order to help the student correct his error without embarrassing him.

✦ ✦ ✦

✦ Rav Shlomo Zalman Auerbach was officiating at a wedding when he noticed a rabbi who had been invited to serve as a witness. Reb Shlomo Zalman felt that some of this rabbi's views bordered on heresy, and he was not comfortable using him as a witness. On the one hand, he was not willing to compromise his standards of truth, yet on the other, he could not shame a fellow Jew. Reb Shlomo Zalman told the rabbi that he would like to honor him with officiating at the wedding, and that he, instead, would serve as a witness. The rabbi was honored with the switch, and Reb Shlomo Zalman was pleased he would not have to compromise.

Plan: ✦ *Make sure to correct other people's misconceptions and errors in their understanding of Torah, while sparing them embarrassment.*

40 GUIDE OTHERS TOWARDS PEACE

מעמידו על השלום

I n the Torah student's pursuit of truth, he often finds himself at odds with his colleagues. Sometimes such conflict leads to a sharp exchange of words. This sharpness, however, does not escalate into personal animosity, and every effort is made to maintain a peaceful and loving relationship (*Midrash Shmuel; Lechem Shamayim*). The Talmud observes that even a father and son, or a *rebbi* and student, can become enemies while in the midst of study (*Kiddushin* 30b). Yet they will not move from their places in the study hall until their love is restored. The differences are not personalized and remain on an intellectual level (*Cheshev HaEfod*).

◆ A woman once saw the Chazon Ish, in his younger years, heatedly arguing in learning with the young Rav Aharon Kotler, the Kletzker Rosh Yeshivah. The woman knew the Chazon Ish to be a patient, soft-spoken person who never seemed to be agitated. When she saw the two red-faced men shouting at each other, she became frightened, and ran to alert Rebbetzin Greineman, the Chazon Ish's sister. The Rebbetzin allayed her fears. "Don't worry," she said, "they are the best of friends, and they will remain the best of friends!" Only moments later, the woman was amazed to see the two scholars smiling broadly at each other.

Part of the Torah scholar's mission is to increase peace in the world (*Berachos* 64a), and he should do what he can to promote peace among others (*Derech Chaim*).

✦ Rav Chaim Volozhin would expend great efforts to restore peace among Jews. He once spent hours trying to reconcile differences between two laborers. A family member remarked that it was not befitting the Rav's honor for him to be involved in such matters. Rav Chaim responded, "Chazal ordained at the end of the *Amidah*, as well as at the end of Kaddish, that one take three steps backwards and say *shalom*. We see that a person must be willing to take a few steps back to make *shalom*, so why should I be concerned about my honor?"

✦ ✦ ✦

✦ Rav Shach was once involved in making a *shidduch*. The young couple married, but shortly afterwards suffered from serious marital problems. When the Rosh Yeshivah heard about the matter, he felt personally responsible and resolved to do what he could to help the situation. Over the next two years, he regularly traveled from Bnei Brak to Jerusalem — almost daily — to spend hours in the couple's home, trying to restore marital harmony.

Despite Rav Shach's advanced age and his tremendous diligence in Torah study, he felt that no sacrifice was too great for the sake of restoring *shalom bayis*.

Another understanding of the meaning of the attribute of "guiding others towards peace" is restoring peace between man and his Creator. Peace is created when people come closer to Hashem through *teshuvah* (see *Derech Chaim*). Rav Moshe Feinstein ruled that just as one must give a tenth of his earnings to tzedakah, so one must also donate a tenth of his time to bringing others closer to Hashem.

✦ In 1914, a group of prominent *rabbanim*, including Rav Yosef Chaim Sonnenfeld and Rav Avraham Yitzchok Kook, traveled throughout the northern part of Eretz Yisrael for a month on a *teshuvah* campaign. They visited many communities in order to strengthen their observance and to help establish Torah schools for the children. More recently, many *gedolei Yisrael* have encouraged young Torah scholars to dedicate some of their time to introducing Torah to their estranged brethren through organizations such as P'eylim and Lev L'Achim.

Plan: ✦ *Ensure that disagreements with colleagues regarding Torah do not degenerate into personal quarrels.*
✦ *Help bring and maintain peace between others.*
✦ *Encourage others to strengthen their observance.*

41 COMPOSING ONESELF IN STUDY

מתיישב לבו בתלמודו

I
t was explained earlier (no. 13) that Torah must be studied with composure in order to be understood properly. This is necessary for one's own understanding. However, even after one has studied, he must calmly and thoroughly review what he has learned, before engaging in discussion with others or offering a ruling (*Derech Chaim; Midrash Shmuel*).

✦ A student of Rav Baruch Ber Leibovitz posed a question to him on his *shiur*. The Rosh Yeshivah thought for a few minutes, and then suggested a profound and brilliant explanation. The student walked away satisfied. A few minutes later, however, Rav Baruch Ber approached the young man and stated simply, "My solution is not true." The student reviewed the Rosh Yeshivah's insight several times, but could find no flaw.

Early the next morning, the student was awakened by a knock at the door. He rose quickly and opened the door, only to find Reb Baruch Ber, whose face was lit up by a broad smile. Reb Baruch Ber excitedly exclaimed, "It is true, after all!" The student was puzzled. "Why did the Rosh Yeshivah think otherwise until now?" he thought to himself. The Rosh Yeshivah continued, "Although I first thought my solution was valid, I was troubled because I didn't see how the correct answer could have come to me so quickly. Only now, after deliberating on it for a number of hours, am I comfortable saying that it is true."

A person must carefully prepare the material he has learned, in order to present it to others in the best possible way (*Tiferes Yisrael*). One may be a great scholar and yet be unable to explain himself to others in such a way that they will understand.

Rav Yechezkel Abramsky would not give a simple *shiur*, even to laymen, without first reviewing the material eight times! Before presenting a *shiur* to yeshivah students, he would review the material twelve times! On one occasion, a student challenged a point Rav Yechezkel made during the *shiur*. The Rav apologized, saying that he had thought of the very same question and he had answered it to his own satisfaction. However, he had not intended to mention the point in the *shiur* and he was not sufficiently prepared to recap his own answer. He would not try to say something in the *shiur* without being well prepared to do so.

✦ ✦ ✦

Rav Nachum Partzovitz said that he would prepare his weekly Sunday *shiur* during the week before. Then, from Friday until Sunday, he would determine how to present the material to his students. Preparing how to deliver the *shiur* is totally different from preparing the *shiur*'s content.

✦ ✦ ✦

✦ Rav Avraham Pam was completely devoted to his students. He once said that in all his years of teaching, he had never had a study session in any *maseches* other than that which his students were studying in the yeshivah.

The Chafetz Chaim explains this attribute homiletically, explaining that one must set his heart according to his study. This means that it is not sufficient to just amass knowledge; one must also internalize the lessons of the Torah. The goal of Torah study is to put one's learning into practice, thereby elevating one's nature.

✦ A young genius boasted to the Kotzker Rebbe that he had already been through half of *Shas*. The Kotzker chided the fellow: "That is fine, young man, but how much of *Shas* has been through you?"

Plan: ✦ *Review studies thoroughly before suggesting a chiddush or ruling.*
✦ *Prepare carefully before teaching Torah to others.*
✦ *Take learning to heart and apply it accordingly.*

42 TO ASK AND TO ANSWER

שואל ומשיב

A
sking questions in order to fully understand the material is an integral part of Torah study. The system of questioning and answering expands the topic and ensures that nothing is accepted as truth without being scrutinized. This process clarifies the material for both teacher and student (*Derech Chaim*). The Mishnah teaches that the student who is too shy to ask will not learn, whereas the teacher whose impatience discourages questions will not be able to teach (*Avos* 2:5).

Rav Yitzchak Hutner highlights the obligation to discuss the Exodus at the Seder in a question/answer format. He explains that information received as an answer to a question is more highly regarded — and better retained — than information simply presented as fact. Often, the answer requires the assistance of the question more than the question requires the answer!

The Torah scholar must learn to ask the right questions. A

good question is relevant to the discussion, not merely a tangential query that may distract from the matter at hand. Tangential questions lead to confusion (*Midrash Shmuel; Lechem Shamayim*). The scholar's questions also show a grasp of the material being presented — that which is central to the discussion and that which is merely incidental. We thus find that the scholar's question is half the answer (*Shiurei Da'as, "Darko shel Torah"*).

> ✦ Rav Shach refused to answer questions about topics he was not currently learning; he actually claimed he was unable to do so. Someone once asked him how it was that he was able to answer questions on a myriad of issues and problems, yet he was unable to answer a question in learning. The Rosh Yeshivah responded that other questions did not require his full concentration; he was able to respond while thinking about the *sugya* he was currently learning. However, questions in learning required his complete concentration, and that would necessitate his ignoring the current *sugya* — something he could not do.

Just as the scholar is encouraged to ask questions, he is also encouraged to answer people's questions. One who does not care to answer will not achieve greatness in Torah (*Derech Chaim*).

> ✦ Rav Shlomo Zalman Auerbach received letters daily from around the world. The letters contained all kinds of queries and requests. As one of the foremost halachic authorities, Reb Shlomo Zalman took his responsibility seriously and responded to the most intricate and complex questions. Once, while perusing the pile of mail, he noticed a letter from a nine-year-old boy, who had written about his difficulty in understanding a *Tosafos*. Rav Shlomo Zalman responded to this query as well. He

explained the *Tosafos* simply and concisely, in a manner appropriate for a nine year old. When asked why he would tax his limited time and strength to answer something that could have been addressed by any yeshivah student, he simply said, "This, too, is Torah, and I must teach it. What difference is there between teaching a great scholar and a young boy?"

✦ ✦ ✦

A student once posed a Torah question to Rav Avraham Pam, Rosh Yeshivah of Torah Vodaath. Rav Pam responded that he would have to research the matter. Two weeks later, when the two met on the street, Rav Pam removed a Gemara from his briefcase, opened to the commentary of the Maharsha, and showed the student the answer to his question. The student was amazed that the Rosh Yeshivah happened to have the right volume at the time. Rav Pam explained that he was hoping they would meet somewhere, and so he had kept the volume with him wherever he went.

The scholar must also answer questions in a clear and concise manner. The Talmud (*Kiddushin* 30a) teaches that one should make an effort to understand Torah so well that he will be able to answer any question succinctly and without hesitation (*Cheshev HaEfod*).

> Plan: ✦ Overcome shyness that prevents asking questions.
> ✦ Focus questions on the subject matter and answer questions in the clearest possible way.

43 TO LISTEN AND TO ADD

שומע ומוסיף

The true scholar does not merely repeat what he has been taught. He uses the methodology he has learned to apply his knowledge to new places, building on the basic principles even further (*Midrash Shmuel*). He is careful, however, not to contradict the words of his *rebbi* (*Rashi*).

Rav Chaim Shmulevitz revealed that every time he had trouble understanding a statement of Chazal, he projected how he thought his *rebbi*, Rav Yerucham Levovitz, would explain it. This is the meaning of a true *rebbi–talmid* relationship. In fact, Reb Chaim resolved a seeming contradiction with this concept: The Talmud says that Rav Eliezer never expressed an opinion he had not heard from his *rebbi* (*Sukkah* 28a). However, elsewhere we find Rav Eliezer expounding ideas "that were never heard before" (*Avos d'Rabbi Nassan* 6). The answer is that although Rav Eliezer may not have heard these exact ideas from his *rebbi*, he had totally absorbed his *rebbi*'s methodology, and so he analyzed everything just as his *rebbi* would have done. (The same insight was also heard from Rav Mordechai Gifter.)

✦ When Rav Chaim Shmulevitz would deliver a *shiur*, he often presented the questions and then the principle with which to resolve the questions. However, the final step in the resolution he would omit, allowing his students to tie up the pieces together. In this way, he trained them to correctly apply the information they had learned. He felt that it is necessary to make one's student a partner in the learning process.

Another interpretation of "listening and adding" is "to listen and to continue listening" (*Midrash Shmuel*). A person who has an unquenchable thirst for Torah, so that he never tires of listening to it, shows the love of Torah necessary for its acquisition (*Ruach Chaim*).

✦ Rav Nachum Partzovitz approached a *chasan* the day after his engagement celebration, and asked him to repeat the piece of Torah he had delivered at the event. The *chasan* was surprised at the request, so Rav Nachum explained. "My father-in-law [Rav Chaim Shmulevitz] was at the celebration and told me that you delivered an important piece of Torah. If that is so, it is important that I hear it, too!" The young man could not get over the great Rosh Yeshivah's love for Torah.

The Talmud relates an incident about Rav Preida, whose student had difficulty understanding the *shiur* (*Eiruvin* 54b). Rav Preida used to repeat his lesson four hundred times in order for the student to understand. The Talmud praises Rav Preida for his endless patience in teaching the student. Rav Chaim Shmulevitz, however, used to say that he was even more impressed by Rav Preida's student, whose love for Torah didn't allow him to become discouraged, despite having to hear each piece so many times!

The more a person listens and delves into Torah, the more he will uncover and find in it. Ultimately, a person will never become bored with Torah, as there is always something new to discover (*Lechem Shamayim*).

Rav Shlomo Wolbe writes that a student's greatest success comes from preparing *chaburos* (Torah discourses) to be shared with his fellow students. It is not necessary for the student to drive himself to think of something novel. Rather, as Rav Chaim Volozhiner explains, when one toils to understand Torah he will inevitably discover a new understanding, and that is called a *chiddush*, a novel insight.

Plan: ✦ *Review lessons repeatedly, trying to understand them better each time.*
✦ *Share insights with others.*

44 LEARN FOR THE PURPOSE OF TEACHING

לומד על מנת ללמד

Torah was not meant to be kept within any single individual's domain; it was intended to be the legacy of every Jew: "*Morashah kehillas Yaakov*" (*Devarim* 33:4). It is each person's responsibility to teach what he knows to others (*Derech Chaim*). The *Sifri* teaches that the command "You shall teach them to your children" (*Devarim* 6:7), refers to teaching one's students. The *Sefer Chassidim* (530) states that one who keeps his Torah insights to himself is guilty of theft, for the insights were only granted him in order that he share them with others.

✦ In his later years, Rav Shimon Shkop was advised by his doctors to ease his gruelling schedule as a Rosh Yeshivah. Reb Shimon, however, refused. He said that

Hashem only grants a person life so that he can accomplish things on behalf of Torah. If he were to stop doing what he was able to do best — teach his students — what purpose would there be to his life?

✦ ✦ ✦

✦ Rav Elya Meir Bloch taught his students that their responsibility was to spread Hashem's glory throughout the world, in the way for which they were best suited. In practice, however, he advised them to remain in the yeshivah to first perfect themselves to the degree they were able. He compared their situation to a soldier going out to war with a pistol, as opposed to going armed with a cannon. Although a student with even a little knowledge could influence others, the effect of a little knowledge — similar to the limitations of a pistol — would be small. The student who spends a longer period developing himself has a much greater weapon in his arsenal, such as a cannon, and can accomplish much more. (I heard this from my Rosh Yeshivah, HaRav Avraham Chaim Levin, *shlita.*)

When one learns Torah not just for himself, but in order to share his knowledge with others, he merits special Divine assistance in understanding the Torah. This is similar to the Talmudic principle (*Bava Kama* 92a) that one who prays on behalf of others will merit to be answered first (*Midrash Shmuel*).

✦ An *avreich* told the Steipler Gaon that he did not feel he was accomplishing much in *kollel*. He asked the Steipler whether he should continue learning in *kollel* or whether he should accept a teaching position. The Steipler lamented that teaching was no longer valued in the same way it had been in earlier generations. It used to be that every *avreich* aspired to be able to teach. When no position was available, he would have no alternative but to continue studying in *kollel*. The Steipler encouraged the fellow to accept a teaching position, adding that every *gadol* from the previous generation rose to greatness through teaching others.

✦ ✦ ✦

✦ Rav Baruch Ber Leibovitz said about himself that any bit of success he enjoyed in Torah study was only the result of his having toiled in helping others with Torah.

Teaching others also helps a person remember his learning better. Each time a person teaches the material, it becomes more deeply ingrained in his mind (*Midrash Shmuel*). Moreover, when one teaches others, they can remind him of his teachings, even if he forgets them himself (*Lechem Shamayim*). The Talmud relates that Rav Yosef took ill and forgot all his Torah. When he began to study again, his student, Abaye, would remind him what he had taught in his earlier years (*Nedarim* 41a).

Plan: ✦ *Draw on Torah learning to teach others.*

45 LEARN FOR THE PURPOSE OF DOING
לומד על מנת לעשות

The study of Torah should not merely be for the purpose of sharpening one's mind, nor for the sake of amassing great knowledge. Torah is the guidebook for our every action in life: both in mitzvah observance and in what appears to be mundane matters, such as eating, sleeping, and conducting business. Studying Torah without the intention of putting it into practice defeats the purpose of its study. As the Mishnah in *Avos* (1:17) says, "It is not the study that is primary but rather the action" (*Derech Chaim*). The *Iggeres HaRamban* suggests that at the conclusion of every Torah session, one should reflect on whether anything was learned that can be integrated into one's conduct and life.

However, this should not be construed to mean that one's study should be limited to learning halachah as opposed to

Gemara, which often deals with the theoretical and the esoteric. Quite the contrary, the study of Talmud is the primary text for most scholars. The intention is that one's study should be for the purpose of sanctifying oneself and bringing oneself closer to the service of Hashem (*Cheshev HaEfod*).

Before entering the field of Jewish outreach, I asked Rav Simcha Wasserman, a Torah giant as well as a successful outreach personality, for some advice in learning with unaffiliated Jews. He said that all areas of Torah have the capacity to influence others, as the Midrash teaches: "The light [of Torah] will return them to good" (*Eichah Rabbah, pesikta* 2). However, only Torah that is accepted as authoritative has this light. Learning halachah with someone who has no interest in observing mitzvos will not be productive, since that person has not accepted the Torah as authoritative. Such study is not considered Torah, and will be devoid of its power to influence behavior. In such a case, it is better to learn an area of Torah that is less practical, and is thus easier for a secular person to believe and accept.

> A principal asked Rav Moshe Feinstein if it would be acceptable to alter the accepted practice, and teach tractate *Berachos* instead of *Bava Metzia* to the younger students, since it has greater practical application. (*Maseches Berachos* deals with prayers, while *Bava Metzia* deals with money matters.) Reb Moshe disagreed. He felt it was important for a child to know that the Torah isn't just for one's conduct in shul, but also has application to one's business dealings. Even what to do when one finds something in the street is governed by the Torah.

Learning for the purpose of putting one's knowledge into practice is also a prerequisite for teaching Torah. A teacher who does not practice what he preaches will never be able to impart Torah to his students (Rabbi Abraham Twerski).

✦ Rabbi Zev Leff relates an incident in which a college professor of ethics was caught in a compromising situation. A colleague expressed his disappointment in the man, whom he considered a hypocrite for teaching ethics while acting unethically. The professor, however, was unrepentant. "I don't have to be an isosceles triangle to teach math, do I? What does my personal behavior have to do with what I teach?" This attitude is the antithesis of how one must behave in order to be a teacher of Torah. The Torah teacher must reflect and incorporate into his own behavior everything he wishes to teach.

Plan: ✦ *Reflect on what can be put into practice after each study session.*

✦ *Keep in mind that learning should bring one closer to serving Hashem.*

46 MAKE ONE'S TEACHER WISER

מחכים את רבו

A student should never be embarrassed to ask questions. Not only are questions beneficial to one's own understanding (as we have said earlier), but they are equally beneficial to the teacher. Questions force the teacher to better clarify the matter in his own mind (*Midrash Shmuel*). The Talmud cites *Rebbi* as saying, "Much have I learned from my teachers; even more have I learned from my colleagues. From my students, though, I have learned the most" (*Ta'anis* 7a). In the same way that little twigs are used to ignite a large log, the young student expands his teacher's knowledge through his questions and comments (*Derech Chaim*).

◆ The Chasam Sofer, in his younger years, was once speaking with the elderly Rav Mordechai Binet. In the course of their conversation, the Chasam Sofer cited a Yerushalmi, which, surprisingly, had escaped Rav Binet. It was a bit of an embarrassing moment. The Chasam Sofer consoled the elderly Rav. He gave an example of two wagons, a large one, laden with all kinds of merchandise and a second, smaller wagon carrying a lighter load. The larger, heavier wagon was difficult to maneuver, and could not turn the small corners, whereas the lighter one had no difficulty at all. Rav Binet's vast knowledge could be compared to the heavily laden wagon. Thus, it was more difficult for him to recall an obscure Yerushalmi. The Chasam Sofer humbly compared his own, more limited knowledge, to the light wagon with the smaller load. Thus, the sections he had mastered were easier to recall.

Another interpretation of "making one's teacher wiser" is that one should believe his *rebbi* to be a great and wise person, mentally placing him on a pedestal. Only when the student feels this way will he be driven to learn as much as he is able to from his *rebbi* (*Midrash Shmuel*). This will also stimulate him to strive harder to understand his *rebbi*'s words — and for any inability to understand, he will blame himself rather than his *rebbi* (*Tiferes Yisrael*). The Talmud says that a student must view his *rebbi* as an angel of Hashem if he is to receive Torah from him (*Chagigah* 15b). *Sefer HaMikneh* (Introduction) explains this as meaning that a student should view his *rebbi* as a model of perfection.

✦ Rav Elchanan Wasserman's respect for his *rebbi*, the Chafetz Chaim, was legendary. He once compared the Chafetz Chaim to a *sefer Torah*. He explained that a child learns the Torah and thinks he knows it. A more mature student learns the same Torah, and thinks he understands its depth. The Torah scholar learns the same Torah, and thinks he understands most of it, except for some difficulties. The great scholar, however, learns the same Torah, and realizes he doesn't begin to understand it! The greater the person, Reb Elchanan said, the more he realizes he can't begin to appreciate the Chafetz Chaim's greatness.

✦ ✦ ✦

✦ Rav Shlomo Heiman delivered a brilliant *shiur* answering a difficult Talmudic question. The students were awed by the sheer genius, yet after the *shiur* the Rosh Yeshivah sighed and said, "Although the reasoning seems flawless, it cannot be so. Rabbi Akiva Eiger posed this question and could not find a satisfactory answer. It is impossible that I could have conceived an answer that escaped the great mind of Rabbi Akiva Eiger."

Plan: ✦ *Engage teachers with questions and comments about their lessons.*

✦ *Appreciate Rebbeim by recognizing their greatness, viewing any lack of understanding as a personal shortcoming.*

47 FOCUS ATTENTION ON ONE'S LEARNING
מכיין את שמועתו

It is important to thoroughly understand what one learns and not merely parrot what one has heard. When a student writes or memorizes what he hears from his *rebbi* without really understanding what was said, the information cannot be well retained, and will be quickly forgotten (*Midrash Shmuel; Derech Chaim*). The Chazon Ish (*Igros 33*) advises students that when learning one opinion in the Talmud or *Rishonim*, they should try to understand the opposing opinions, and why it is that they disagree with the present opinion. The main growth in Torah comes from challenging an opinion rather than from agreeing with it, since by challenging it, the essence of the opinion is defined.

✦ When Rav Yaakov Kaminetzky came to enroll in the yeshivah in Slutzk, he spoke with the Rosh Yeshivah,

Rav Isser Zalman Meltzer. In the course of their conversation, he started talking about a dispute between the Ramban and the Ba'al HaMaor in *Bava Kama*. Reb Isser Zalman stopped him and said, "I don't appreciate *'shalosh seudos Torah,'* traditionally said in the dark, when nobody can check out anything that is being said, and the speaker can say anything he pleases! Please bring me a *sefer*, so we can see the Ramban's actual words and try to understand what he means."

The Chazon Ish writes that errors made by incorrectly comparing and applying Torah principles are much more damaging than those made by not knowing the material itself.

Another understanding of the attribute of "focusing on one's learning" is to concentrate all one's attention on the specific point being raised. In the same way that a concentration of light rays creates a laser beam that can penetrate solid objects, mental concentration allows for the penetration and probing of the deepest parts of Torah (Rabbi Abraham Twerski).

✦ Rav Shach was known to concentrate so deeply that he was totally oblivious to everything around him. Family members once smelled smoke in his apartment. The Rosh Yeshivah had begun to prepare broth for his ailing wife. He was stirring the pot over the fire while concentrating on a complex question. The water cooked out, the pot burned, and smoke began pouring out of the pot — yet Rav Shach continued stirring the pot, his face flushed with concentration, oblivious to the smoke all around him.

One should also be precise when repeating his *rebbi's* words and not change them at all, in accordance with the Talmud's directive to always repeat his *rebbi's* words verbatim (*Berachos* 47a). When a person is careful to preserve the exact words, he will better remember them. Furthermore, if the person does not understand the words properly, another scholar may be able to decipher them correctly; whereas, if the words are changed, that may not be possible (*Cheshev HaEfod*).

The Talmud (*Pesachim* 42a) relates that Rav Masna taught the city folk that the matzah flour for Pesach may only be kneaded with *mayim shelonu*, water that is drawn and left overnight to cool. The people, however, misunderstood him as saying they must use "*mayim shelanu*," meaning "our water." They pressed Rav Masna for some of his water — until he clarified his words. The Talmud does not relate the story to mock the foolishness of the city folk, but rather to express admiration for their complying with their teacher's precise words, despite the illogic.

> *Plan:* ✦ *Concentrate and remove extraneous thoughts when studying.*
> ✦ *Analyze the material to understand it clearly.*
> ✦ *Be attentive to the rebbi's precise words.*

48 CITE ONE'S SOURCES BY NAME
אומר דבר בשם אומרו

O
ne must give credit where it is due and cite
the source for a teaching. One who plagia-
rizes another person's insight and calls it his
own will not be able to acquire Torah, since
he is trying to dishonestly gain what is not
his (*Midrash Shmuel*).

✦ Rav Chaim Shmulevitz was careful to cite the source
for any new insight he heard or saw. In his later years,
when he was no longer able to remember the source for every insight, he was careful to acknowledge that the insight
was not his own.

One reason for this concern is that one who is meticulous
about citing each source will likewise be meticulous in the lesson
itself (*Derech Chaim*). The Talmud is extremely careful to cite
each source, sometimes taking as many as five lines or more to do
so: for example, where Rav Reuven made a statement in the name

of Rav Shimon, who cited it in the name of Rav Levi, etc. These painstaking measures are necessary to guarantee the integrity of the transmission of the Sinaitic tradition. The *Panim Me'iros* (see Introduction) suggests, however, that one who is a *talmid muvhak*, a primary student, need not cite his *rebbi*, since it goes without saying that whatever he espouses stems from his *rebbi*. This is also implied in the Talmud (*Yevamos* 96b).

Another reason for supplying the proper source is that each person was granted his own specific portion in Torah. It is important to know from where each piece of Torah originates, because it is an expression of that individual's allotted portion. The Talmud (*Gittin* 6b) relates that even Hashem cites Torah opinions in the name of their authors (*Derech Chaim*).

> ◆ A student cited a statement from the Gemara in the name of Rav Huna in front of a recognized Torah scholar. The scholar corrected the student that the statement was made by Rav Pappa, not Rav Huna. Upon checking the source, the student found the scholar to be correct. "How do you remember the names like that?" the student marveled, "I have a difficult enough time remembering the statements!" The scholar responded, "I'll explain the difference between you and me. When you learn a Gemara stating 'Rav Ploni says this and this,' you see the statement being made as Torah. When I learn it, however, I see the words 'Rav Ploni says' also as a part of Torah. Thus, I am careful to recall that, as well."

When one quotes Torah in the name of its author, he brings pleasure to the author, even if he is no longer living. The Talmud (*Yevamos* 97a) states that the lips of the deceased move when their words of Torah are repeated[1] (*Lechem Shamayim*).

---

1 The *Lechem Shamayim* suggests that this might be what the *Beraisa* means, that one who repeats something over in its author's name brings

✦ Often, when a student would speak in learning with
Rav Naftali Trop, the Rosh Yeshivah would suggest various *sevaras* to help the young man develop an approach to explaining the *sugya*. Later, Rav Naftali repeated these ideas in the student's name so many times that the student began to think that he had indeed thought of these ideas himself.

Another reason for citing the proper source is that a particular person often follows the same line of reasoning in various areas of study. By acknowledging the proper author, one can better understand other comments and ideas by the same author (*Ruach Chaim*).

✦ A student mentioned an insight from the Pri
Meggadim to Rav Isser Zalman Meltzer. Reb Isser Zalman challenged the student. He said that given the Pri Meggadim's methodology and approach to learning, he would not have come up with such an insight. When he checked the source, the student realized he had misunderstood the insight.

Plan: ✦ *Be careful to give credit where it is due.*
✦ *Quote the correct sources.*

redemption to the world. The redemption might refer to the idea of learning Torah even while in the grave.

49 CONCLUSION

The *Beraisa* lists the forty-eight qualities necessary to acquire Torah. However, as mentioned earlier, Rav Simcha Zissel Ziv, the Alter of Kelm, recommends one more step: to bring the forty-eight attributes together.

It may be a valiant and admirable endeavor to acquire and cultivate each characteristic, one day at a time, in sequence. But each of these behaviors is incorporated into a whole — one individual, one personality. They must become intertwined parts of a single entity.

We can compare the integrated body of the forty-eight attributes to the physiology of the human body. The body contains various systems. It needs each of these, in order to function. The respiratory system, for example, allows a person to inhale oxygen, while expelling carbon dioxide. The digestive system breaks the food down into its necessary components, while separating the waste to be excreted. The circulatory system carries the blood throughout the body (and with it, of course, the oxygen that is supplied by the respiratory system). Each system works in conjunction (and ideally, in harmony) with the other systems. Although each may function autonomously on some level, all the physiological processes are interrelated. All are necessary for a healthy body.

✦ Rav Chaim Shmulevitz once visited his uncle, Rav Avraham Yoffen, Rosh Yeshivah of Novardok. Reb Chaim asked his uncle to name the brightest student in the yeshivah. Rav Yoffen pointed to one young man. Then Reb Chaim asked which of the students possessed the greatest fear of Heaven. Rav Yoffen pointed to a different student. When asked to identify the yeshivah's most diligent student, a third young man was indicated.

Finally, Reb Chaim asked Rav Yoffen who was his best student. To Reb Chaim's amazement, his uncle pointed to yet another young man. The Rosh Yeshivah explained that although this particular student was not necessarily the best in any one area, he nonetheless surpassed the other students when it came to integrating all of the other qualities.

In telling this story at a later date, Rav Chaim remarked that this fourth young man grew up to be Rav Yaakov Yisrael Kanievsky, the Steipler Gaon — one of the greatest Torah leaders of his time.

Rav Chaim Mordechai Katz, Rosh Yeshiva of Telshe, remarked that although a yeshivah may not have produced a *gadol* in any specific area of Torah, the yeshiva itself, as a composite of greatness — in Torah scholarship and its application, kindness, prayer, and fear of Heaven — is a *gadol*.

In the same way, the forty-eight characteristics must be integrated into a unified whole — one person, one personality — for the acquisition of Torah. The forty-ninth day of the program, and the forty-ninth day of the *omer*, is reserved for each of us to review all the qualities together, to conceptualize bringing them together, and to see them as a seamless tapestry. May we merit to master the forty-eight qualities and thus acquire the Torah!

GLOSSARY

Acharon (pl. *Acharonim*) — Later commentator(s) of Torah and Talmud, beginning from the fifteenth century.

Amora (pl. *Amoraim*) — The rabbis of the Gemara.

avodah — Service of Hashem.

Avraham Avinu — Our forefather Abraham.

ba'alei mussar — Ethical masters, primarily of Rav Yisrael Salanter's school of thought.

bachur — A young man, often referring to a yeshivah student.

beis midrash — A house of study where Torah is learned.

ben Torah — A Torah personality.

bench — Bless; blessing recited after eating a meal (Yiddish).

Berachos — A tractate of Talmud dealing with prayer.

birkas kohanim — The special blessing offered by the *kohanim* on behalf of the Jewish people.

chabura (pl. *chaburos*) — An essay(s) of original Torah insights, generally shared with a small group of friends.

chasan — Groom.

chavrusa (pl. *chavrusos*) — A study partner.

Chazal — An acronym referring to our Sages of Blessed Memory.

chazan — Cantor who leads the prayer service.

cheder — A school where Torah is taught to young children.

chiddush — An original Torah insight.

Chumash — Five Books of Moses.

da'as Torah — An outlook that completely reflects a Torah way of thinking.

davening — Praying.

derashah (pl. *derashos*) — An inspirational Torah speech.

emes — Truth.

Eretz Yisrael — Land of Israel.

Gan Eden — Paradise.

Gedolei Yisrael, Gedolim — The great Torah leaders of each generation.

Gemara — The Talmud.

get — A Jewish divorce.

halachah (pl. — halachos) — Jewish law.

Hashem — G-d (literally, "the Name").

Kabbalah — The mystical level of understanding Torah.

kal v'chomer — A logical inference used to interpret Torah; a fortiori.

kedushah — Holiness.

kinyan (pl. *kinyanim*) — Legal form of acquisition.

kohen (pl. *kohanim*) — Jewish priest(s).

kollel — A full-time study program for married students.

leining — Torah reading.

lashon hara — Negative speech about another person.

ma'ariv — Evening prayer.

maggid (pl. *maggidim*) — Itinerant preacher(s).

malach — Angel.

maseches — A tractate of the Talmud.

Mashgiach — Spiritual supervisor of a yeshivah.

maskil — A follower of the so-called Enlightenment, a movement that spurned Torah.

mesorah — The transmission of the Oral Torah from generation to generation.

minchah — Afternoon prayer.

minyan — Quorum needed for prayer services.

mizrach — Lit. the eastern wall, traditionally the front seats of honor in a synagogue.

mussar — Words of reproof; a program involving the study of Jewish ethical texts, founded by Rav Yisrael Salanter in the nineteenth century.

muktzah — Rabbinic ordinance prohibiting the handling of objects that are not to be used on Shabbos.

oleh — Person called to the Torah for an aliyah.

Olam HaBa — The World to Come.

onan — The status of a mourner before burial; he is precluded from fulfilling any positive mitzvos.

pasken — To issue halachic rulings to queries.

posek — Halachic authority

Rabbeinu — our master and teacher; a title used for Moses.

rebbi — A Torah teacher; a name used to refer to Rabbi Yehuda HaNasi, editor of the Mishnah.

Rebbetzin — Wife of a Rav or Rosh Yeshivah.

Rishonim — The early commentators of the Torah and Talmud, who lived between the eleventh and fifteenth centuries, including Rashi, Rambam, Rosh, and more.

seder (pl. *Sedarim*) — A study session.

sefer (pl. *sefarim*) — A Torah book(s).

sevara — Logical inference in Torah study.

shalom bayis — Domestic peace and harmony.

shalosh seudos — The third Shabbos meal, eaten late Shabbos afternoon.

Shas — The entire order of the Talmud.

Shechinah — The Divine Presence.

shidduch — Matching a couple together for purpose of marriage.

shiur (pl. *shiur*im) — Torah classes.

shochet — A ritual slaughterer.

shtender — A small lectern or podium, used by students in the yeshivah.

shul — Synagogue (Yiddish).

simchas beis hasho'eivah — A joyous celebration held during Sukkos.

siyum — A celebration marking the completion of a part of the Torah, usually a tractate of the Talmud.

sugya — A topic of Torah studied in depth.

talmid — A Torah student.

talmid muvhak — A primary student, who gains the majority of his knowledge from a specific rebbi.

Talmud — The recorded parts of the Oral Tradition, redacted in Babylon around 400 C.E.

Tanna (pl. *Tannaim*) — Authors of the Mishnah, *Beraisa*, and Midrash, around 200 C.E.

Tanach — The combination of Torah, Nevi'im, and the Kesuvim.

Targum — Ancient Aramaic commentary on Torah written by Onkelos.

tefillah (pl. *tefillos*) — Prayers.

teshuvah — Repentance.

Tosafos — A school of *Rishonim*, headed by Rashi's grandchildren.

tzaddik — A pious and righteous man.

tzedakah — Charity.

yarmulka — Skullcap.

Yerushalmi — The Jerusalem Talmud, redacted in Israel at around 300 C.E.

yetzer hara — The Evil Inclination.

zechus — Merit.

zemiros — Religious songs sung at the Shabbos or *yom tov* table.

180

BIOGRAPHICAL
SKETCHES

RAV YECHEZKEL ABRAMSKY — d. 1974; Dayan in London and later in Israel, disciple of Reb Chaim Brisker, author of *Chazon Yechezkel* on *Tosefta*.

RAV AVRAHAM MORDECHAI ALTER — Gerrer Rebbe, d. 1948; rebuilt Ger Chassidus in Israel after the Holocaust.

RAV NAFTALI AMSTERDAM — d. 1916; leading *mussar* personality and Rav, disciple of Rav Yisrael Salanter.

RAV SHLOMO ZALMAN AUERBACH — d. 1995; leading halachic authority and Rosh Yeshivah of Kol Torah in Jerusalem.

RAV ZELIG REUVEN BENGIS — d. 1953; Rav of Eidah HaChareidis in Jerusalem.

RAV NAFTALI TZVI BERLIN — Netziv, d. 1893; Rosh Yeshivah of Volozhin, Lithuania, author of *Ha'emek Davar* and more.

RAV ELIYAHU MEIR BLOCH — d. 1955; founder and Rosh Yeshivah of Telshe Yeshivah in Cleveland.

RAV BENTZION BRUK — d. 1987; Rosh Yeshivah of Novardok, Jersualem.

CHAFETZ CHAIM — Rabbi Yisrael Meir Kagan; d. 1933, leading sage and scholar, lived in Radin, Polandu, author of *Mishnah Berurah* and more.

CHAZON ISH — Rav Avraham Yeshaya Karelitz, d. 1953; halachic authority and leader of Torah Jewry in Israel.

RAV ELIYAHU ELIEZER DESSLER — d. 1954; leading *mussar* thinker, author of *Michtav MeEliyahu*, Mashgiach in Gateshead, England and later in Ponovezh.

RAV ELIYAHU DUSHNITZER — d. 1949; Mashgiach of Lomza Yeshivah in Petach Tikvah, disciple of Chafetz Chaim.

RABBI AKIVA EIGER — d. 1837; Rav of Posen, Prussia, leading Torah authority, author of many *sefarim*.

RAV MOSHE FEINSTEIN — d. 1986; Rosh Yeshivah of Mesivta Tiferes Yerushalayim, leading halachic authority, author of *Igros Moshe* and more.

RAV NOSSON TZVI FINKEL — Alter of Slabodka, d. 1927; founder of Slabodka Yeshivah and Chevron, leading *mussar* thinker.

RAV TZVI PESACH FRANK — d. 1961; Rav of Jerusalem.

RAV MORDECHAI GIFTER — d. 2001; Rosh Yeshivah of Telshe Yeshivah, Cleveland.

RAV ELIEZER GORDON — d. 1910; Rav of Telz, Lithuania, founder of Telshe Yeshivah.

RAV AVRAHAM GRODZENSKI — d. 1941; Mashgiach of Slabodka Yeshivah.

RAV YISRAEL ZEV GUSTMAN — d. 1991; Rosh Yeshivah of Netzach Yisrael, Jerusalem.

RAV YEKUSIEL HALBERSTAM — Klausenberger Rebbe, d. 1994; spiritual leader in D.P. camps and in the rebuilding following Holocaust.

RABBI SHLOMO HALBERSTAM — Bobover Rebbe, d. 2000; rebuilt Chassidic community in Brooklyn, NY after the Holocaust.

RAV SHLOMO HEIMAN — d. 1944; Rosh Yeshivah of Torah Vodaath, disciple of Rav Baruch Ber Lebovitz.

RAV YITZCHAK HUTNER — d. 1981; Rosh Yeshivah of Rabbeinu Chaim Berlin, Brooklyn, NY and Jerusalem, disciple of Alter of Slabodka, author of *Pachad Yitzchak*.

RAV YOSEF SHLOMO KAHANEMAN — Ponovezher Rav, d. 1969; founder of Ponovezh Yeshiva in Bnei Brak.

RAV YAAKOV KAMINETZKY — d. 1986; Rosh Yeshivah of Torah Vodaath, Brooklyn, NY, leading Torah authority, disciple of Alter of Slabodka.

RAV YAAKOV YISRAEL KANIEVSKY — Steipler Gaon, d. 1985; Torah leader in Israel, author of *Kehillas Yaakov*.

RAV AHARON KOTLER — d. 1962; Rosh Yeshivah of Slutzk and Lakewood, NJ, leading Torah authority, disciple of Alter of Slabodka.

RAV CHAIM KREISWORTH — d. 2003; Rav of Antwerp and Rosh Yeshivah in Jerusalem, son-in-law of Rav Avraham Grodzenski.

RAV BARUCH BER LEBOVITZ — d. 1939; Rosh Yeshivah of Kaminetz, disciple of Rav Chaim Brisker.

RAV YERUCHAM LEVOVITZ — d. 1936; Mashgiach of Mir, Poland, author of *Daas Chochmah U'Mussar*.

RAV ELIYAHU LOPIAN — d. 1970, Rosh Yeshivah in London and Mashgiach in Kfar Chassidim.

RAV ISSER ZALMAN MELTZER — d. 1954; Rosh Yeshivah of Slutzk, and later Eitz Chaim in Jerusalem.

RAV SHRAGA FEIVEL MENDLOWITZ — d. 1948; Torah pioneer in America, Menahel of Yeshivah Torah Vodaath and founder of Torah U'Mesorah.

RAV MOSH MIDNER — d. 1929; Menahel of Slonimer Yeshivah in Baranovitch.

RAV AVRAHAM PAM — d. 2001; Rosh Yeshivah of Torah Vodaath, Brooklyn, NY.

RAV NACHUM PARTZOVITZ — d. 1987; Rosh Yeshivah of Mir, Jerusalem, son-in-law of Rav Chaim Shmulevitz.

RAV PESACH PRUSKIN — d. 1939; RAV AND ROSH YESHIVAH OF KOBRIN.

RAV YISRAEL (LIPKIN) SALANTER — D. 1883; FOUNDER OF THE *mussar* movement.

RAV SHIMON SCHWAB — d. 1995; Rav of German Jewish community in Washington Heights, New York.

RAV ELAZAR MENACHEM MAN SHACH — d. 2002; Rosh Yeshivah of Ponovezh, Israel, and leader of Torah Jewry in Israel.

RAV SHIMON SHKOP — d. 1939; Rosh Yeshivah of Grodno, Poland.

RAV CHAIM SHMULEVITZ — d. 1979; Rosh Yeshivah of Mir, Jerusalem; son-in-law of Rav Lazer Yudel Finkel.

RAV MOSHE SOFER — d. 1840; Rav of Pressburg and leader of Hungarian Jewry, author of Chasam Sofer.

RAV CHAIM SOLOVEICHIK — d. 1918; Rosh Yeshivah of Volozhin and Rav of Brisk; son of the Beis HaLevi.

RAV YITZCHAK ZEV SOLOVEICHIK — d. 1959; Brisker Rav, son of Reb Chaim.

RAV YOSEF DOV SOLOVEICHIK — d. 1892; Rosh Yeshivah of Volozhin and Rav of Brisk, author of *Beis HaLevi*.

RAV YOSEF CHAIM SONNENFELD — d. 1932; Torah leader and head of Edah HaChareidis in Jerusalem.

RAV PESACH STEIN — d. 2003; Rosh Yeshivah of Telshe, Cleveland.

RAV AHARON LEIB STEINMAN — contemporary leader of Torah Jewry in Israel, author of *Ayeles HaShachar*.

RAV NAFTALI TROP — d. 1930; Rosh Yeshivah of Radin.

VILNA GAON — Rav Eliyahu Kramer, d. 1779; renowned Torah genius and sage, author of works on all of Torah.

RAV CHAIM VOLOZHINER — d. 1821; disciple of Vilna Gaon, founder of Volozhiner Yeshivah, the prototype of the modern yeshivah movement.

RAV ELCHANAN WASSERMAN — d. 1941; Rosh Yeshivah of Baranovich, disciple of Chafetz Chaim.

RAV SIMCHA WASSERMAN — d. 1992; leading Torah educator in Israel and United States, son of Rav Elchanan Wasserman.

RAV SHLOMO WOLBE — d. 2005; Mashgiach of Yeshivah Be'er Ya'akov, profound thinker and author of *Alei Shur*, son-in-law of Rav Avraham Grodzenski.

RAV AVRAHAM YOFFEN — d. 1970; son-in-law of Alter of Novardok, Rosh Yeshivah of Novardok in Russia, New York, and Israel.

RAV SIMCHA ZISSEL ZIV — d. 1898; one of Rav Yisrael Salanter's foremost disciples, known as the Alter of Kelm.

In loving memory of
Eva Vilensky
יוכבד בת מיכאל
by Alan and Judi Vilensky

לעלוי נשמת
ר אלטר ניסן יעקב בן ר׳ יצחק אייזיק
Jacob (Jack) Gevovich,
By Stuart and Jennifer Mintz
And Mendy and Rebecca Gevovich and
Family

In memory of
Sam Feig
שמואל בן ר׳ מרדכי צבי
by his loving family

In memory of a good friend
who brought joy to many.
Marvin Goldberg
משה יוסף בן אהרן דוד הלוי

In loving memory of

Father
Herbert Harris MD
חיים בן דוד

Grandparents
David Harris דוד בן יחיאל
Yetta Harris יטא בת שמעון מאיר הכהן

Jack Rotner יעקב בן אברהם
Sylvia Rotner שרה בת דוד
Jack Feldman יעקב בן דוד

May this *sefer* bring an *aliyah* to their
neshamos.
Moshe and Sydney Harris and family

In memory of
Ruth W. Ross,

רות בת יצחק הכהן
by her children Alan, Miriam, and Eileen

In memory of
ברל פישל בן יעקב קלטר